ADVICE TO A YOUNG BLACK ACTOR
(AND OTHERS)

ADVICE TO A YOUNG BLACK ACTOR (AND OTHERS)

CONVERSATIONS WITH DOUGLAS TURNER WARD

Gus Edwards

HEINEMANN
Portsmouth, NH

Heinemann
361 Hanover Street
Portsmouth, NH 03801–3912
www.heinemanndrama.com

Offices and agents throughout the world

The author and publisher wish to thank those who have generously given permission to reprint borrowed material:

Photos of Douglas Turner Ward and Gus Edwards taken in December 2000 by Jeffrey W. Miller. Reprinted by permission of photographer.

Photo from *In the Shadow of the Great White Way: Images from the Black Theatre* taken by Bert Andrews, published by Thunder's Mouth Press. Reprinted by permission of the Estate of Bert Andrews.

Photo of Douglas Turner Ward in army uniform, taken by Bert Andrews. Reprinted by permission of the Estate of Bert Andrews.

Photo of Douglas Turner Ward seated on sofa, engaged in conversation with an actor, taken by Bert Andrews. Reprinted by permission of the Estate of Bert Andrews.

Library of Congress Cataloging-in-Publication Data
Ward, Douglas Turner.
  Advice to a young Black actor : conversations with Douglas Turner Ward / Gus Edwards.
    p. cm.
  ISBN 0-325-00665-2 (alk. paper)
  1. Acting—Vocational guidance. 2. African Americans in the performing arts. 3. African American theater. 4. Ward, Douglas Turner—Interviews. 5. Actors—United States—Interviews. I. Edwards, Gus. II. Title.

PN2055.W35 2004
792.02'8'023—dc22   2003024645

Editor: Lisa A. Barnett
Production: Vicki Kasabian
Cover design: Jenny Jensen Greenleaf
Cover photograph: Jeffrey W. Miller
Typesetter: Argosy
Manufacturing: Steve Bernier

Printed in the United States of America on acid-free paper
Sheridan 2019

CONTENTS

CONTENTS

PREFACE

The initial idea for this book came out of a workshop I conducted (for over ten years) at Arizona State University for ethnic students who wanted to explore the possibilities of a career in theatre and, by extension, motion pictures and television. We met for three hours on Saturdays. During the first hour, we had theoretical discussions about playwriting, career management, design, history, any and all aspects of theatre that came up. During the second hour we identified and addressed the ethnic artists' place in all this. The third and final hour was devoted to lessons in acting, which is what most of the students attended the workshop for in the first place. We did exercises, read plays, and ultimately presented an evening of monologues, scenes, and short plays at the end of the semester.

The ethnic background of these students varied, but most were African American. This was not surprising, since I am black and my professional experience comes out of black theatre, mostly my association with the Negro Ensemble Company (NEC) in New York. The students were also mostly beginners—young, energetic, eager, and hungry for information and insight into this profession that can bring satisfaction and (sometimes) glory, fame, and great financial rewards to those who succeed in it. They worked hard, read plays, memorized dialogue, and asked questions. Questions, questions, questions. But the main question black students asked was, *Where can I get a book that speaks directly to us, as African Americans, about acting?*

I browsed my bookshelves, made suggestions, recommended a few titles. But none of them seemed adequate. I looked through publishers' catalogs and searched through libraries, but the kind of book they were looking for just didn't exist. That's when I decided to write one. After all I had been an actor, writer, educator, and director at various times in my life. I further decided that this book would be the kind of book I'd have liked to have had when I arrived in New York City in 1959, passionate about embarking on an acting career. (The amazing thing is that in all the intervening years no book of the kind has been published.)

I sat down and began to write. The original title was *Acting Is Truth,* and I formulated a series of chapter titles covering all or at least most of the questions I had been asked. I hoped to compress all I had come to know about acting after more than thirty years of being involved with it in one way or another into a slim volume that would not overwhelm the reader by its size.

I also wanted opinions more informed than my own. Opinions from people who had done it successfully and who were well known for doing it. So I made a list of the people I knew. In that list was Douglas Turner Ward. He's done it all: write, direct, produce, act. And he'd done it all with such precision and well-developed skill that both he and the company he cofounded (the NEC) have won every major theatrical award this country gives for excellence in theatre. Who better to speak to about this book? Who better to collaborate with on it?

So, in the spring of 1995, while on sabbatical, I went to New York and embarked on a series of audiotaped conversations on the art of acting (from a black perspective) with Doug Ward. Our conversations took place in Doug's little corner office when the NEC was located on Forty-sixth Street, on the fifth floor overlooking Broadway. Generally he would arrive around 6:00 P.M. when everyone (secretaries, production people, etc.) had already left the premises. I would usually get there a half hour ahead of him and wait. Sometimes I'd read a magazine; other times I'd make notes and ponder what questions I was going to ask or what direction I wanted our talk to take. I always assumed the role of the novice or beginner seeking advice, information, or direction: "Suppose I were a young black person of let's say seventeen or so who decided that I wanted to be an actor more than anything else in the world. What would you tell me? What pointers could you give me? What advice could you provide about auditions . . . acting workshops . . . my experiences as a black person . . . sustaining long runs . . . creating a character" . . . whatever. I tried to ask my questions in the simplest way in order to elicit clear and simple answers that would be comprehensive to the untrained or nontheatre person. And always I had a small tape recorder that I would put, between us, on his desk.

When he arrived, we would greet each other and engage in a bit of chitchat; then the real conversation would begin. Doug would sit at his desk with his back to the window. I would sit on the other side, from which vantage point I could see the lights of Broadway in all their gaudy and garish splendor. We would talk until I felt we had exhausted the subject, between two and two and a half hours. Then we'd leave and go to one of the bars on Eighth or Ninth Avenue, have a drink or two, and talk about more secular things like women, world affairs, whatever.

I ultimately wound up with something like twenty hours of tape, or nearly three hundred transcribed pages. Nothing was orderly. We had just talked. I asked questions, Doug answered, elaborated, sometimes argued, other times was provocative and insightful. I read the transcripts over and over, but I couldn't make heads or tails of anything we'd talked about, at least nothing that would fit into the schematic pattern I had envisioned for *Acting Is Truth*. So I abandoned the project and moved on to other things.

But I kept the tapes and the transcripts. Who knew? Perhaps they might prove useful in another context. Four years passed before I moved all the material out of my office at home into the garage. The step after that, when the garage became too cluttered, was to take it to the dumpster. I was on the verge of doing just that when another voice inside me said, "Give it another look and *then* dump it." So I did.

I realized I had been exhaustive in my questions and that Doug had in turn been extremely thorough in his responses. Of course our talks hadn't fit with what I had written for *Acting Is Truth*. The voice was too distinctly Doug's. So I decided to let Doug have the floor. The result is the book you're holding. I am still part of the enterprise but in a supporting role.

The new title is entirely appropriate. It directly states what the book does: share the advice of one very talented and distinguished man of the theatre, particularly black theatre.

DOUGLAS TURNER WARD AND THE NEC

Douglas Turner Ward's personality is outsized and his conversational manner boisterous. He is highly opinionated, argumentative, and forceful in the way he presents himself and his ideas. When standing next to him, I'm often surprised that he's not a physically bigger man, because he gives the impression of size, immense size. Not that he's small. He's 6'1". But I often think of him on the scale of someone like Paul Bunyan or some equally mythic figure. I think this stems from the bigness of his ideas.

One has only to talk to him for a short while to realize that this man is a visionary who is also insightful, provocative, daring, and astute. His knowledge of American and world theatre past and present is encyclopedic. He is also single minded, stubborn, and blunt. That he is a controversial figure is not surprising, because Doug Ward is totally uncompromising when he feels strongly about something.

"If any hope outside of chance individual fortune exists for Negro playwrights as a group, or, for that matter, Negro actors and other theatre craftsmen, the most immediate, pressing, practical, absolutely minimally essential active first step is the development of a permanent Negro company of at least Off-Broadway size and dimension. Not in the future . . . but now."

With those words, written in 1966 as part of an article entitled "American Theatre: For Whites Only," Ward, a former journalist turned actor and playwright, hurled a gauntlet into the face of the American theatrical establishment concerning the role of African American actors, directors, playwrights, and other craftsmen. His was not the first voice to protest the way blacks were being segregated and presented in mainstream American theatre. There had been many others before who spoke out. But perhaps the timing of the article—and the fact that it appeared in the *New York Times*, one of the most respected and influential newspapers in America and abroad—contributed to its impact.

But one must also credit the urgency and power of Ward's language in the article, starting with the title. In approximately three thousand words, Ward first pinpointed the state of American theatre in the 1960s, calling it "A Theatre of Diversion . . . whose main problem is not that it's safe, but that it is surpassingly irrelevant." Then, with the speed and power of an express train, he discussed the nonexistent status of the black (Negro) playwright and theatre artist in the American landscape and called for the creation of "an all-embracing, all-encompassing theatre of black (Negro) identity" suggesting that "just as the intrusion of lower-middle-class and working-class voices reinvigorated polite, white English drama, so might the Negro [or African American] artist infuse life into the moribund corpus of American Theatre."

The response to this article was immediate. Days after it appeared, Ward, along with two associates, Robert Hooks and Gerald Krone, was invited by W. McNeil Lowry (1913–1993), of the Ford Foundation, to present a proposal for the formation of a theatre company that would address the needs outlined in the article. That company was the Negro Ensemble Company, or NEC, at one time the most successful, talked about, written about black theatre company in America.

During the stewardship of Ward as artistic director and overall producer, from 1967–1993, the company presented close to eighty main-stage productions and hundreds of staged readings and gave a start to the careers of many of the best-known African American actors in America theatre, films, and television. It also introduced a host of black playwrights, not only from America but the world over, including two Nobel Prizewinners, Wole Soyinka and Derek Walcott. The company has contributed such popular titles as *Home, A Soldier's Play, The River Niger,* and *Ceremonies in Dark Old Men* to the enduring body of American theatre literature. Its collection of awards includes thirteen Obies, four Vernon Rice awards, two Clarence Derments, the NAACP Image Award, an Edwin Booth

Award, two Tonys, and one Pulitzer Prize. There are also awards from Australia, Ireland, Bermuda, Germany, Italy, and London.

Large achievements are so rare in our time that often when they appear they go unrecognized. Genuine heroes, too, walk among us. But our idea of what constitutes a hero has been so debased by fraudulent history and the tabloid press that when one comes along and touches our lives, we usually fail to recognize that individual until after they've passed on. Douglas Turner Ward is to my mind one of those heroes, one of those giants who walked among us and changed our lives in significant ways. Yes, some of what he accomplished has been recognized and acknowledged via honorary doctorates and various other awards. But the largest part of what he achieved still goes unheralded. And that is probably because not many people know that he is the one who did it.

Sure, everyone knows he visualized and ran the NEC for nearly thirty years. Some might dispute the way he ran it perhaps, but none will deny that he did in fact run it. But what is not talked about—and perhaps is not known—is that Douglas Turner Ward helped teach America to see—to see the color and ethnicity of its own population. Before Ward came along, worthwhile theatrical works (plays) were frequently rejected as being "too ethnic." The operative phrase applied to any culturally specific work hoping for artistic validity and an audience larger than its author's immediate community was "crossover appeal." The success of Lorraine Hansberry's *A Raisin in the Sun* was attributed to its having great "crossover appeal." Movie actor Sidney Poitier's supposedly "crossover appeal" explained why he was so popular.

Ward took great issue with that phrase. "You mean to tell me," he would ask both in private and public forums, "that a play which intimately speaks to the lives and concerns of five or fifty thousand black people has to be considered worthless because five or fifty or five hundred white people can't relate to it? I can't accept that. And anyone who does is full of you know what."

He proved the rightness of that statement by creating the NEC and developing an audience for it. An audience of African Americans whose lives, history, and values were reflected and echoed in the plays the NEC produced. He then took the idea one step further. He challenged America's most popular media—motion pictures and television—to present America as it is, not how they would like to pretend it ought to be.

"I don't care where you go in this country," he would say, "even in the deepest part of the South, you're going to see Chinamen, Latinos, black folks, and others working in supermarkets, restaurants, laundries, and all kinds of places. Films that don't employ minorities to reflect that are white fantasy works that have nothing to do with the real world we live in." To illustrate that point, he regularly employed many white, Asian, and Hispanic people to work on stage and off at the NEC. And all speak well of their experience with the company.

In time, movies and TV began to take notice and eventually things began to change. Of course Ward was not solely responsible. Rights groups, theatrical unions, and other voices had been clamoring for more accurate representation as well. But Ward was one of its most vocal champions and, besides talking, he was practicing what he preached.

In his 1987 article "Counterpoint: A Twenty-Year View of Black Theatre," which was written at the request of the *New York Times* as a bookend to his 1966 article but which they refused to publish once they'd read it, Ward sums up the NEC's achievements: "For two decades, the NEC provided an institutional base for black participation. It gave programmatic thrust to multiple artistic objectives. It offered the mechanism for actualizing ambitions. It nurtured talent and ability, encouraged risk taking, and gave expression to the controversial. The range and scope, variety and complexities of its productions were prodigious, shattering all notions of black drama being singular in style, form, and content, proving that black writers hardly share a common point of view, sensibility, means of expression, thematic interest, or world vision. . . . And no matter the future, what has already transpired is ineradicable. Black artists did it. . . . Their collaborators were black audiences. . . . They catalyzed and sustained activities of remarkable scope and depth. They more than justified my prediction that if given the opportunity, they would change the complexion and 'infuse life into the moribund corpus of American Theatre.'"

In the Beginning

WHAT IS ACTING?

What exactly is acting? How does it differ from performing? How are stage acting and film acting similar and how are they different?

There probably is a more apt schoolbook definition somewhere that I never thought about, but acting to me is a representation of the whole spectrum of life—the re-creation and representation, the individual and group communication, of lived and imagined human behavior. In that sense, the individual actor or a group of actors become the representatives of a lived experience, the depiction of which is as significant and important as not only any other form of media communication but any other professional endeavor. So at its highest evaluation it is a craft, a skill, and everything else worthy of the highest respect—whatever we value in terms of human advancement and relationships. The very expression of it requires a full commitment and skilled training to achieve mastery, like any other important occupation or craft. At its highest, it's not something that you do spontaneously without thought, without calculation, or without finding out how or be creative, without any practice, education, or training.

I always emphasize this in order to distinguish between what we call *performing* and *acting*. We commonly witness representations and behavior constituting what we call *performance*, starting with the fact that children playact. We all at some point indulge in play. It even exists in animals. We pretend, we imagine, and then we playact based on our need to imitate what we've seen, what we've observed, in others. It is how we learn. We learn to become adults by imitating the behavior of our parents and other people around us. So there's a universal basis for acting that is natural. It starts with our behavior as children, and ultimately it is re-created or represented in a higher

3

form of expression, in a formal way, through various communication media: film, stage, TV. That aspect of spontaneous behavior is always there, it is common, and it is shared in some sense by the performer, the actor, and anybody who is involved in communicating.

But very often there's confusion between what's performance, what's behavior, and what's acting. And that's why I'm trying to find a way to make a clear distinction. Yes, there's a common perform-ance aspect shared by anybody who communicates through behav-ior or through imitation, who is asked to be representational in communicating. And then there is the actor, and the term *acting*, which is to me the higher form in which the individual becomes the vessel for re-creating the complexity of human behavior—the psy-chology of human beings and their relationship with one another, their relationship to the world, their relationship to themselves, and their expression through imagination of how we involve ourselves in particular situations. This is a skill that has to be obtained con-sciously through training and experience.

It is not comparable to the exploitation of what I consider real behavior—meaning that I can, let's say, with a camera, capture on tape or film some vivid images of somebody expressing herself, record a personality that lends itself to being vivacious or captivat-ing. The difference is that the latter can be done with what we call nonactors, as was demonstrated in many instances during the period of neorealism in Italian films. In films like *The Bicycle Thief* and *Open City*, DeSica and the great Rossellini used nonactors and cre-ated compelling poetry about the social environment and society at the time. The nonactors, or the nonprofessional actors, gave com-pelling behavioristic performances that rang true to life. And cer-tainly those classics show that with the right sort of leadership, guidance, suggestiveness, or control on the part of a director you can get behavioristic performances even from nonprofessional actors that in their own right can be as compelling as those from the so-called professional actors, who consciously through calculation, craft, and skill re-create a believable character or person within a scripted situation and lead us to both believe and be involved in the truth of what they represent.

Now, all of us in this business are performers, whether we are professional or nonprofessional actors. That remains common. And

4

that remains a fact we can all relate to. I try to make a distinction between the performer and the actor only to try to make a distinction about what goes in and what is both common and not common.

Take, for instance, the contrast between, let's say, a performer, particularly in the mass media, and a trained or developed actor. An actor has the command of a certain craft and skill to consciously, calculatedly depict a believable result that particularly in relation to the context of the stage, takes a certain amount of trained expertise to pull off. The stage actor can modify or modulate a performance and accomplish a similar thing on film. The opposite is not necessarily true of someone who is not trained in this way. I'm speaking of film performers, even very advanced film performers, who have also gained a certain skill and craft for expressing and communicating within a visual medium. Those same performers often cannot come and do the same thing on stage. A lot of people don't understand that. And that's why a lot of times when film actors who have had no background in the theatre suddenly are asked to appear on stage and create a more complex image of anybody other than their star persona, they can't. That's why a lot of times film actors who come to act on stage will fade into the scenery after ten minutes. All of the stardom, all of the close-ups, all of the technology that can take advantage of what they bring as wonderful film performers, does not work on stage.

While just the opposite is true of the stage actor. The adjustment to film is primarily a technical adjustment. A lot of people make a mistake and say, well, the actor on stage is too big. No. There's nothing inherent about stage acting that cannot be readjusted to the frame and the magnification of film. On film you will not need the projection, you will not need all the technique elements to be functioning in a scene, as you do on stage, where you have to address the shifting attention of audiences and hold the attention of the people in the third balcony. You must both reach them vocally and be sufficiently physically expressive to hold their attention. With film, a camera, and a recording mike, you don't really need that magnification. The technology does it, and therefore you have to readjust some of those elements of projection to the technology.

In many instances the film actor who starts off merely as a personality or an untrained performer, after great exposure and the challenge of adapting to the technical and unique artistic elements of film, will begin to develop some of the same interpretive skills that are the bread-and-butter possessions of a stage actor. Look at the maturation of a Kirk Douglas or a Bert Lancaster. It was not a great surprise, but it was very interesting for me to work with Kirk Douglas in *One Flew Over the Cuckoo's Nest*. I mean, he held his own with a very strong group of stage-trained actors—Gene Wilder, William Daniels, and others. There were no lightweights in that cast. Kirk hadn't been on stage in almost forty years. He was right for the role of McMurphy, of course. But it wasn't just a movie star up there. He definitely wasn't just relying on the familiarity of Kirk Douglas in that sense. But by that time, through working in film, he not only had acquired a mastery of film craft but also had deepened to the point that in approaching a dimensional characterization on stage, he brought weight and depth to it. I never saw Bert Lancaster in a stage play, but watching the movie work from this former circus gymnast and so forth, he was a very remarkable actor.

So what I'm saying is that the acquisition of craft and skill is not just some formal thing. It is that which is finally achieved recognizably—in other words, when you see it. And it is more than just behavior. It is an acquisition of craft and skills that give you the ability to make something memorable and even profound out of a role or characterization. And that to me is what real acting is all about.

WHERE TO BEGIN?

If a young black person of seventeen decided that he or she wanted to be an actor, what would your advice be?

At that age I'd tell them, in the first place, they should seek and plan for their education. Continuing their education. At that age, seventeen, they are probably on the verge of college. My advice would be to continue to get a good liberal arts education, especially designed to expose them to subjects beyond what they've already learned in high school—literature and all associated subjects, including philosophy and political science. They need to be first given the foundation of a broad liberal education in literature, drama, poetry, and so forth. These courses, while not necessarily yet focused on the nuts and bolts of acting, are the things that begin to shape your thoughts and your sensitivities. They begin to provide you with that which ultimately enables you to then deal with the various aspects of acting once you narrow yourself down to studying the tools and craft of the profession. You should have the background of a cultivated education. And I don't mean cultivated in the superficial bourgeois meaning of the word, but sophisticated knowledge about what has existed in man's attempt to engage in artistic communication. That's what a basic education should require. It's not easy, because a lot of times the formal business of receiving this in college is so routine that it's almost counterproductive. But ideally, this is what I would say to them.

Now while you are doing that at seventeen, I would then say—whether you get it in the same setting or whether you have to get it in addition to your regular studies—you should also begin to study what I call the muscles or the tools of the discipline, the elements that can be abstracted and learned for themselves. That's dance, music, singing, and, wherever you can get it, good solid speech training that enhances and broadens your ability to express yourself verbally in a wide and flexible variety of speech patterns. So that your tongue and your lips and everything related to those muscles get to be trained to speak well. Not well in the sense of correct bourgeois standards, but to speak well in the sense that you can handle language, the language of a script, any script, expressively. Since an actor ultimately is called on to represent characters from many different backgrounds, classes, and nationalities, that's the beginning standpoint.

If you notice, I haven't put any emphasis on so-called acting training per se. I think at that age if you are doing these other things and you can then get into participatory acting situations—workshops or groups that put on plays—this will be sufficient to introduce you to the task of communicating through interpretation. At seventeen one's mental capacity and felt life experience usually are not very advanced. There's not very much to act *from*. All you do is imitate. Like when you see little children get on stage and imitate adults. They mime adults. When you see a little five-year-old get up and do a discotheque dance, they are imitating what they see grown-ups or older kids do. But that's just a hollow imitation, because they haven't even reached the stage to know what the hell twisting their waist is really about. By the time you are seventeen you begin to know what the twisting is about, but you still don't have the life experience to be able to use it in any meaningful way.

What I said earlier, you've got to equip yourself for interpreting the sum total of human experience. But you're not even close to being able to do that at the age of seventeen. You are just beginning to live life in a mature adult way. You are just beginning to reach the age where you are now going to start becoming totally responsible for yourself. You are now beginning to be independently responsible. And until you actually cross over into maturity and take full responsibility for yourself, you do not have too much that you can interpret with any degree of authority or conviction.

Oh, you can act the surface of behavior and so forth. That's always possible. When one looks at those child actors who grow up in films or a TV series, what we are seeing essentially is not so much a practiced or conscious craft, we are seeing a child's natural ability to perform and to show off, which is present to one degree or another in all children. Some children are just more open and adept at it than others. But we're not seeing actors as actors yet. That's why a lot of times suddenly, after those same child actors become grown, they have such problems. Real-life problems. All they have behind them is the imitation of life through show biz. And then when they are faced with real maturity and responsibility, they don't know how to cope with the mature behavior required of them. All of it gets mixed up and they don't know the difference between real life and play life. Those things get all merged together and they get confused, until finally they go and sometimes do destructive things. You see, you are not really able to start studying real acting until you get beyond the age of playacting. I would start from eighteen more or less, because that's when you are beginning to reach that stage I was talking about. There are exceptions, of course. But not many.

It's only when someone reaches the stage where they are responsible for their own real-life behavior that they can start studying how acting operates in a craft way in terms of being able to depict or interpret life. So, I'll say it again: a *good* liberal arts education would be a solid foundation for a later career in acting.

ACTING AND COMMITMENT

In theatre, the word commitment *is always being thrown around in a loose and imprecise fashion. So I put it to you. What does* commitment *or* total commitment *mean in terms of playing a character or interpreting a role?*

Total commitment means that I start from the premise that the project is worthy and the professional demands it makes are worth it. Then I am totally committed to what the project requires of me. If it demands representation of the broadest range of human experience and behavior, concerning situations both real and imaginative, then I can commit myself seriously to being a vessel for contributing in my area, which is performing. That is my role in the enterprise, and I am committed fully to doing it. If it's not exploitative, if it's not consciously sensationalizing, then my commitment is total. I commit myself to realizing the aims of the particular project or production to the point that I'm willing to go on using myself to the fullest extent, physically, emotionally, and psychologically. I do whatever I have to do to achieve that aim. And I always say that my only proviso in terms of what I won't do is, there's no reason to ever consciously hurt anybody on stage or literally perform a sexual act. But beyond those two disclaimers, there are no taboos. Although I won't hurt anyone, I will absolutely, physically play the most lacerating negative, even reprehensible character, and work out the believability of the physical violence to give a greater illusion of it than if we did it real. The same with the sexual thing—the most unerotic thing in the world is a live sexual act. As soon as you see somebody perform a conclusive sexual act on stage, it becomes something else. The suspension of disbelief is out the window. And the point of the play will be lost.

I use only these examples in relation to commitment because, unfortunately, even in our modern-day theatre, people think of wanting to be actors with a lot of taboos about what they will and won't do. I tell them, then you don't want to be an actor. Because if you come to my audition saying, my religious or political views won't allow me to do certain things, then I can't use you, because the intent of my work is to represent human existence in some truthful ways so as to communicate to us and, I hope, make some contribution about how we live with and function among each other. If that is the objective and you have all of these other devotions, commitments, or what have you that prevent you from doing the job, then why bother? The profession has its own demands, what I call serious intentions, aims, and ambitions, that are equal to any other profession or role in society, including preachers, politicians, psychologists, whatever. I consider our purpose equal to their purpose. They have different needs and demands to follow, and so do we.

NATURAL TALENT

I hear actors talk all the time about talent. Recently I had a young black actor come to me and say, "I know I have a lot of natural talent. Raw talent. My teachers say I do. And other people do, too. So why do I have to get more training? Isn't natural talent enough?" What is your response to that? Is there such a thing as natural talent? And does that naturally talented person need to be trained like everybody else?

Is there such a thing as "natural" talent? Yes, there is. But what that is, I couldn't define. Just for discussion sake, I think we all have various degrees of what is called *talent*. It just exists and goes in different directions for different individuals. Some people have a talent for music. Some people are idiots in every other way but then have this talent for one given thing, such as mathematics. In other ways they almost can't function. I don't know why that is, I just know that it exists.

We talked earlier about reflecting, communicating, and interpreting in theatre. We know that somebody excites us or enlivens us when they can do that. Or when they can do degrees of it. Sometimes it could be fragments of it. Some people will have a surface ability to mimic patterns of behavior. Like some people can immediately do dialects. Those are only superficial aspects of ability, but they show to one degree or another how it exists in a diversified way. The people with great acting talent are those people who are able to do all the things we are talking about with a depth that we respond to. They have a grasp and an ability to communicate it in a way that we feel or sense has an element of profound truth about it. They are able to perform and do it with a depth that rivets our attention or draws us in to relate to them as if they have shown us new insights being communicated in a fresh and urgent way for the first time.

I think from that height of deep ability or deep talent, if you want to call it that, it narrows down in scale. Some people are able to perform to a supreme extent, and some people can only manage a narrow range, and so forth. But nevertheless training is needed, if only to show the actor how to harness and control that great natural or raw talent he or she might possess. This allows the actor to modulate, shape, and channel this talent in potent and effective ways.

In summary, I would have to say, yes, there is such a thing as natural talent. But it has to be coupled with training for it to be truly effective.

ACTING ESSENTIALS

If I were to ask you to break acting down in a nutshell, in just single words that could be put in a list to serve as a guide or outline to be filled in later, what would those words be?

Acting in a nutshell breaks down to this:

Observation

Discipline

Concentration

Life experience

Imagination

Daring

Words (those we speak)

Listening (the words we hear)

Analyzing wants and needs

Much of acting involves reacting to what is said and listening each time as though it is the first time. And you learn to act only by doing it. And doing it often.

Acting and Being Black

Actor or Black Actor?

Tapping into the Black Experience

Black Speech and Accents

Political Correctness

ACTOR OR BLACK ACTOR

Let's talk about acting and being black or African American. Is this something one should be consciously aware of, or something one should ignore? Is it an advantage or a disadvantage? One hears so much about searching for a universality that makes us all share common, thus recognizable, traits. Also, one hears a lot about color and color-blind casting. What is your take on all of this? And how should a black actor use or not use this in the business of creating a character and playing a part?

My contention here, and I've been on a mission about this for a while, is that the natural route to learning the craft of acting involves your imagination. Do whatever else later but first start out and deal with what you know and have experienced, what you've heard, things like that. Don't start out fantasizing as a beginning step. The route to opening your imagination is to first access it through the concrete specifics of the known, the heard, the experienced, and so forth. What you start out with in acting is basic. Yourself. The only vehicle for acting is you—your body, your mind, your experiences in life. No agency other than yourself. And since you will start from there, you have to start from that which is most familiar to that self. What you know, what you experience, what you've heard.

Black actors exist in broad, various ways, crossing many lines of class and circumstantial experience, but essentially, in our American context, we have been shaped by a unique experience that happens to be common to other black people in other parts of the world because of the diaspora. Having some earlier link to Africa is a common historical/cultural experience that transforms itself, that crosses boundaries. I mean you could say those blacks brought to the West Indies, those brought to Brazil, those brought to the

United States, all share a history of subjugation, disfranchisement, et cetera, that has created a common existential background. That is what's closest to us, whether we like it or not, whether we try to escape it or not.

What I'm talking about is first dealing with the known. If you want to be an actor you're going to have to deal with self. You're going to have to deal with that particular history of self. There's no way that one can represent, interpret, any experience except from the nature of one's consciousness. And one's consciousness is not a blank slate. It is based on what one has experienced. And what we have experienced in the Western Hemisphere in particular is the primacy of the historical black experience. You will have to start with those ingredients that go into that as a temporal experience and ultimately get to its roots historically.

If a black person wants to become an actor, the route is an exploration of self. And exploration of self is to explore the roots of your day-to-day experiences within the family, within the context of your environment, within the psychology of your personality and whatever goes into that. That is the starting point. That gives you the access to the commonalty of how to relate to everybody else. But the first thing you have to start from is that self, and that's not a blank sheet.

Now this is not a precious possession in terms of some mystical blackness. That's not what I'm talking about. No. It's a very concrete, historical experience. Take me, for example. I come from Louisiana. I was born in Louisiana and I was born in a particular context; in my instance, it was a plantation. The people who were my relatives run the gamut of a particular kind. But the commonality that is on both sides, my mother, my father, my grandparents, their historical experience—all of it goes back, as far as we can trace it, to slavery, if you want to put it that way. And to whatever has been inherited culturally, the food, the religion, the music. All of these things are components of that background. So if I'm going to learn how to be expressive, first and foremost I have to investigate all that is common to that past, that shaped it, that shaped my consciousness, too. I have to go into that first if I'm going to try to be truthfully expressive through interpreting what constitutes that legacy. In very definite ways I have to deal with that first and foremost.

We also have to understand that when it comes to something like speech, all actors are going to use the same muscles. They have to be flexible of tongue, appreciate the nuances of tonal modulations, et cetera. All actors, white, black, or green, have to deal with those basics. But when you talk about interpreting characters, there will be a particular rhythm to the cultural experience. I am not going to be believable playing a Russian before I can first play my grandfather. That is going to give me closer access to the character of my own experience. I will come to find out after playing my grandfather that my grandfather's experience might be similar to those of the peasants of the Gulag, or pre-Czarist Russia, during Turgenev's time. But I'm not going to be able to do anything with Czarist Russia, I'm not going to be able to do anything with Chekhov, until I know what those peasants down on the Southern American plantation were like. I can't skip over that experience and say, I'm going to be a Chekhovian actor. I can't play Chekhov worth a damn unless first I come at it through the route and particularities of my own subjective personal/historical experience. It is not separate; it is related. It gives me access. It is first things first.

But I know that unfortunately in a racist society things get turned ass backwards. All over the country, including the place where I taught most recently, you see this error being compounded. You wouldn't believe how many young blacks are being taught to be everything else but themselves first. It got to the point at the school where I was that even a member of the debate team came to me and said that when they participate in these debate competitions the white teachers tell the black actors they don't want them to do anything from black works, because that's too easy for them. They want them to do something more difficult. So I asked, do they ever tell the white kids at the same competition that they shouldn't do white works because it's too easy for them? They told me no. It never occurred to them that it's the same thing.

They tell black actors not to do *A Raisin in the Sun*. Again, because ostensibly it's too easy for them. Do they tell the white actors not do Tennessee Williams because it's too easy for them? No, they don't. That's not the same thing as far as they're concerned. In the first place, this view is a misapprehension. Nothing is easy for an actor to do. Creating or developing a character in a

19

dimensional way and then communicating it to an audience is a very difficult task.

None of this would be worthy of comment if its negativity wasn't so destructive, if things weren't so turned around. It is assumed that black people should be exploring everything but who they really are. Because deep down underneath, there's a devaluation of black life and black history. That's the bottom line. And this devaluation then infests and infects the thinking of even blacks themselves. Therefore they devalue themselves, they devalue their own material, they devalue their own lives, they devalue their own characters. And psychologically this cripples their being able to interpret anything. Because denial cannot empower you to do anything well.

Any black actors out there talking about, I want to play universal characters, meaning white people, before they play themselves, is sad and painfully misguided. It's an absurd undertaking, because it's not possible. They're not going to be able to do others better than they are able to do themselves and the people who informed their own direct experiences, especially during their formative years. Anyone with any knowledge of what interpretive work is all about knows this is true, white or black.

The smart people all over the world, even those in Eurocentric cultures or power centers, would want me to play their czars and their kings and their peasants, their broad spectrum of characters, because they see me playing the Johnny Williamses and the Russell B. Parkers and the Bob Tyrones of *The River Niger, Ceremonies in Dark Old Men,* and *The Offering.* They will want me to play those roles because they see what I'm best in. They're not going to come and get me to play their roles because they hear me acting out some silly rhetorical imitation of a character to whom I have no cultural ties. I would dare say right now as an actor they would hire me to play Ivan the Terrible not because they want me to play some artificial imitation of a Russian, but because they see the power, skill, anger, irritability, frustration, or whatever that I bring to play Johnny Williams in *The River Niger* and say, God, that would make a great Ivan, and they would be right.

When you heard Paul Robeson sing, it was obvious that Paul Robeson, in a nonracist environment or even if he had been able to live in Russia, would probably have been one of the greatest interpreters of some of the great Russian operas—Mussorgsky, for instance. I once heard Paul do an excerpt from *Boris Godunov* and it was great. Just like it's now been proven with Leontyne Price and Shirley Verrett and all those divas. You think that it's any accident that the majority of major opera divas in the world today are black? Do you think they were really hired to be the divas in all of those great roles because somebody came and saw them try to be something they weren't? No. It is what those singers bring to those roles out of the depth of their own culture, despite the fact that they're singing basically European modes of art. It is the deep-down element of the artist coming out of her roots and the whole life experience that Leontyne brings to her roles. It is what the best of them bring. That's what causes them to match their talents to the requirements of whatever they sing. They are not being some whitewashed, whiteface version of somebody else or some other culture. No, they are being who they are and tapping into where they come from. So the source, the starting point of acting is not a mystical thing, but something very pragmatic. You start from the basis and the concreteness of your own life and your own experience. From there, you have access to everything else.

Culture is very specific, creativity is very specific, artistry is very specific. It's not some vague, evanescent sort of liberal nonsense about color-blind casting. There's no such thing. As I've said often, I guess when you don't see color the only color you see is white. If you're color-blind, then the only color you'll see is white. That's what everybody would like you to think—that when you are color-blind, you'll wind up seeing nothing but white. There's no such thing as color-blindness. Not in my view. Awareness of differences doesn't make things superior. There's no experience that's superior to another. But at least in order for everybody to be equal as a starting point, one has to acknowledge the primacy of one's own specific cultural background.

TAPPING INTO THE BLACK EXPERIENCE

my job as a white director of Black students too

Can you elaborate on this for me please?

Sure. The special thing that the black actor has to tap into—and it has to be a conscious act, because unfortunately everything about the history of the society he lives in is designed to devalue it—is his own experience. Organically he shouldn't even have to think about it. Unfortunately he has to—a black actor almost has to make a conscious, willed decision to be himself, if you want to put it that way, to use his own life and his own experiences as the starting point of whatever he brings into his training and his work.

He has to use and explore his own background. You have to remember that just like anybody else, to find out what he's doing through action and objective acting exercises, he has to use particular experiences out of his own background. Now, in a lot of instances he doesn't have all of these nice little neat bourgeois contexts to draw from. The white kid comes to class and does an exercise about, let's say, cleaning up his room. His momma told him that if he didn't clean up his room he wasn't going to be able to go to a ball game. That white actor is thinking about a room that he got at ten years old, by himself, because his sister's got one next door. In cleaning up his room, he's dealing with a space and room full of toys and everything else.

Okay, now you take a black actor out of a shack, housing project, or inner-city ghetto somewhere. When *he* does that exercise, he might say he didn't have a room. Take me. I don't remember having a room to myself until I was almost in my twenties. I grew up in a household where there was an old woman living in the same space I had. She was in the bed and I was on the cot. So cleaning up my room or doing that exercise when I was at that age requires a different sense of how I will do it and use it. I have to bring to the exercise the reality that I didn't have a room full of toys to be dealt with. I had specific things I had to do because of the class, the context, and the economic factors that were part of my youth. All of these factors have to be accepted and used in creating circumstances and scenes around one's own life and experience.

Black actors or aspiring black actors have to investigate their particulars to the extent I'm talking about. And they have to relish doing it in every way. Because they have advantages, in the sense that certain elements of their life experiences may have given them one-up-manships in some of the actor's expressive tools. They may have been brought up in backgrounds and environments where music was so pervasive, surrounded their everyday life to such an extent, that they've not so much been imbued with natural rhythm, but achieved a musical sensitivity by osmosis. They've already been sensitized in certain areas because of the nature of their culture. They've already been conditioned in very special ways because of economic circumstances or the circumstances of the world they inhabit. Maybe it's the threatening element of the world that surrounds them. They can't take safety for granted like a bourgeois white kid. Walking on the street or going into certain places, they are conditioned to develop a second set of ears, keep a second set of eyes trained behind them. There are all kinds of elements of reality that give them different sensitivities they have to employ and use.

But they must rid themselves of the incrustation of ideas about their inferiority and the inferiority of their lives, their experiences, and their relationships that has been superimposed on them. They have to throw that shit out and do the opposite. Since their actual experience equips them to be more in tune to the palpable reality of their world, they have to glory in starting to use and empower themselves from that premise. They should accept the fact that, if anything, the accident of their own personal background and experience already gives them greater sensitivities to real life than maybe some of their white compatriots, who most likely, through class advantages or ignorance, have more illusions about both life and their place in the world.

Again, this is not some mysterious advantage. Every advantage I'm talking about that a black actor or a black interpreter can bring

is use of trauma?
w/o trauma

forth is provided by the concrete reality of life. Like it or not, we have seen throughout the history of art that very often those put into an existential relationship with life and its hardships, who have already faced difficult realities imposed on them, whether through dominance, oppression, or what have you, have been provided with a depth of comprehension and feeling they merely need to tap into, explore, and let prevail through their art.

This is all that I mean when I say that black actors, potential actors, and so forth have natural advantages if they will use them. The problem is that the advantage is being turned into the opposite. They have been overwhelmed and self-devalued till they tap into and believe the opposite. In other words, they see their background and experiences not as an advantage, but as a disadvantage. And therefore they don't explore or take advantage of what rightfully could and should be advantages in a particular field, acting, where you are supposed to represent and interpret life.

Who is better equipped to do that than those who have already faced the reality of life at its sometimes most negative point? People who only see life through rose-colored glasses are less equipped to see it in its real dimension, because they are drawing on their illusions about it. Generally, those who have faced life in its negative realities have no illusions about what we call human behavior and experience. We know what it can be at its worst and also at its best. And when you know what it is at its worst, it's such a relief to feel some elements of it at its best, until sensuously and intellectually you understand both sides of it and can communicate those feelings in vital and urgent ways.

BLACK SPEECH AND ACCENTS

What about the particular cadences and inflections common to the way many black people speak?

I just came back from doing a workshop in Florida. Mixed in with the college group were some eight- and nine-year-old kids. They sat in on the sessions, which was strange. I thought, wait a minute, why am I talking to eight- and nine-year-olds? But their teacher brought them in, so I accepted them, and they were very well behaved. But they didn't necessarily grasp and probably weren't even interested in some of the things I was talking about. And I knew that. Nevertheless, I addressed everything I had to say to everyone. Including those kids.

At the end, when they had to leave, their teacher asked them, "Would you like to ask Mr. Ward a question?" And one kid says, "How do you deal with the accents in *Day of Absence*?" And I almost fell out of my chair. Here was a sensible question from a kid I thought was just sitting there being polite, but not listening. It turned out these eight- and nine-year-old kids are doing my play *Day of Absence.* So I said, "Don't worry about it. No, don't worry about it at all. Just talk naturally and that will be fine."

I went on to explain that even with professionals sometimes, in dealing with the black idiom or accents and things like that, actors tend to want to lay too heavily on them. And suddenly they're enunciating it, stressing the written phonetics. And you say, Wait a minute. Wait a minute. You're putting too much emphasis on the written idiomatic thing. It doesn't sound natural. All those phonetic points were in the writing. And all the writer was suggesting was the underlying rhythm. Ear and eye are not commensurate.

Oral and written are not necessarily compatible. You don't have to become a slave to phonetic diction. Just get the suggestive flavor, and that's all that'll be necessary if the rest of it is truthful and emotionally lived.

POLITICAL CORRECTNESS

Positive/negative . . . negative/positive. These are words we hear ad nauseam in relation to black life and black theatre. What's your take on it?

The words *positive* and *negative* have been severely misused in theatre. Many people talk to me about it and have no idea what they mean. But then they come into interpretive acting and some say, I only play roles that are positive, or, I won't play roles where I kiss anybody. I think the line has gotten blurred to the extent that people think that you can legitimately be a so-called actor and have your wants, your dos and don'ts. It's like having somebody come to an audition and before you can tell them what to do, they say, Well, first let me tell you what I don't do. I don't do anything without my scarf on my head because I'm a Muslim woman. I don't play any parts unless I got my head covered. Or, I don't do anything that requires me to say goddamn. Or, I don't do anything with any profanity. Without even finding out what the play is all about it's, I don't do this and I don't do that. Some people think that they can think of being actors and really legitimately consider those kinds of objections valid. Well, I don't.

Those people are not actors. No, to me they're imposters. And if they get away with it, it's because the environment has enough crap out there that some people don't know where common sense begins and political correctness should end. So you might be able to find your niche and get away with doing that nonsense for a while. But you're not an actor, at least not in my definition of the word. My feelings in terms of the function of an actor, I repeat, is that it's equal to any other function, including involvement that contradicts or seemingly goes against your belief system—your selected belief system.

27

Let's put it this way, the task, the interpretive function that I'm talking about, is continuous for an actor. It's permanent. You could be a born-again Christian and tomorrow you could reverse yourself and go back to being an atheist, let's say. So every time you willfully change a religious belief, do you change your dos and don'ts about acting? No, acting is a permanent commitment. You can change your politics, you change your religion, and so forth.

So what I'm saying here is, your religious conviction, your political conviction, should not have any determination as to what you do and you don't do in a narrow sense. In some religions there are certain days where you're not supposed to do this and do that, because you're fundamentalists or orthodox. Once you open that door to accepting these taboos, where do you stop? Suppose you wind up with a cast of fifteen people, and each one of them has a different prohibition about time: I can't be here on Friday; I can't do anything on Sundays. It would just be a disaster.

I was speaking at a black school in South Carolina some years ago and everybody was telling me how much they wanted to be in theatre, and then at a workshop or something I was conducting people were telling me, Well, I can't be in it, because I've got to go to church on Sunday and the time conflicts. And I said, Well, you won't be in theatre. We can't have that in theatre. You've got to choose coming to the theatre. Now, I wasn't trying to be rigid. But religions have to be flexible enough to incorporate other aspects of life. You never hear people talk about how their religion keeps them from going to work. Do you know anyone with a religious belief that says it doesn't allow them to work? So you say, Wait a minute, why is it that all of these prohibitions don't really interfere with making a living? Finally I told them theatre has its own needs and schedules and sacrifices. And then you try to get them to see the point: *It seems to me that church is always going to be there. We're only doing this show for two weeks. What is the big deal about you not being able to go to church for this one Sunday when you're going to go to church for the rest of your life.* Theatre has its own priority that people don't want to accept.

A lot of people are now being political in terms of being black, employing what I call the pseudobourgeois debate about *positive* and *negative*. Some actors literally say, Why do I have to play a *negative* black character? And you almost want to say, Do you know what drama is? I mean, the whole description of drama. The term is self-explanatory; it's conflict. How are you going to have conflict without positive and negative? If you're only going to play the positive, who is going to play the negative? All of you want to play the positive and no one wants to play the negative. Once again it comes down to, What do you want to do? How committed are you? Now, somebody is going to say, Damn, you are a purist aren't you? Yes, because I believe that this profession, its function, and what it contributes are important to the world and society. And because of that, to me its requirements and demands must be given equal weight and value with all the other activities and professions out there.

not about erasing identity, but about giving theatre the same weight as all other aspects of our lives. We make plans around our work schedules why would theatre be any different?

Studying Acting

Acting as a Profession

Acting Training

The Validity of Workshops

*The Stanislavsky System,
or Method*

ACTING AS A PROFESSION

Talk to me about acting as a profession—what it is and how it should be approached.

Acting to me, ultimately, if you're going to do it seriously to the extent that I'm talking about, should be something you have to do. It is something you need for self-expression in some deep way that is going to cause you to put forth the effort and energy to do it well. And then be able to stay with it in the face of all of the negative frustrations that you may encounter in trying to make a living at it. So it is absolutely something that you must need to do.

Now, I think all people have a certain amount and degree of talent. But I would say that only people with a serious need to express whatever that talent is should try to stick with it. Not get turned off because of external reasons of not being in control of the work that you're going to get or not get. But acting is too wearing, too difficult, too potentially frustrating an endeavor to pursue frivolously or casually, unless you just want to do it as a sideline while you do other things. Acting is a very serious endeavor.

The interesting thing about me is that I went to study it for other reasons. I figured it would help me as a writer. But what I knew and was mature enough to understand right away was that in order to find out what acting was about, I had to deal with it and focus on it as if I wanted to do it exclusively. So I studied acting not just as a means of helping myself as a writer, I studied it as if that was the only thing I wanted to do. I committed myself to it fully while I was studying it. Now I still hadn't made up my mind whether to pursue it as a profession, but I went through the process of studying as if it was exclusively what I wanted to do. Consequently, I gained a solid grasp of the required skills even before I mentally committed to doing it.

But I found, despite my lack of conscious commitment to it as a profession, that in the process of gaining the skills and craft, that I also *needed* to do it. And therefore it wasn't enough just to involve myself in it as a sideline. And what was proven over my long career is that the fulfillment of some of the challenges of acting has provided me with many of the greatest feelings of achievement that I've ever had. Compared with other things I've done, it's equal to any other fulfillment. Those great moments feeling that I've succeeded in my performing or acting goals justifies the fact that I have spent so much time trying to learn and master it.

So, my short answer is: acting as a profession must be approached seriously, diligently, and with as much energy as you can muster.

ACTING TRAINING

All right, so I want to be an actor. It is the profession that I have chosen to dedicate all my energies and time to. I want to be an actor, a star, or just somebody who earns his living doing this full time. I want to interpret and reinterpret some of the great parts and perhaps even create a few new ones before I'm through. But first things first. I need to get training. Where should I go? And what should I, an aspiring black actor, look for?

The training of black actors today in academia and in acting schools is ass backwards. I think I said that before. I mean most of the schools don't even use black material. Could you imagine a bunch of actors going to college for four years and not even studying a piece of their own material? Not one character that might be remindful of their own experience or somebody they might know? And yet they're asked to do everybody else's characters. Can you imagine getting some kids out of the ghetto and they start out by doing Tennessee Williams's *The Glass Menagerie*? Can you imagine it? That's almost laughable. But I've seen it done in so many places of supposedly higher education that the laugh sort of sticks in my throat.

But it's a problem that has to be addressed and has to be addressed now. Black students have to demand works that come out of their own specific background and culture: black American literature, black American dramatic literature. And if the teachers don't know it, they have to make them aware of it. And if the teachers refuse, then they have to look elsewhere for their education and training. It's as simple as that.

THE VALIDITY OF WORKSHOPS

What about workshops? Let's say I can't afford to go to a college or university. Or, for whatever reasons, I don't want to go to any of those places. I want to go to a workshop. Someplace like the one Paul Mann conducted that you attended. There are many being advertised in the trade papers and other places that are more within my budget. How can they help me? And what should I look for?

The existence of workshops was helpful to me. There were no active theatre companies at the time willing to take on novices in a meaningful way. Especially black ones. There were no stable or standard companies of a kind where one could get on-the-job experience. There wasn't a thriving theatre world where, as in the British system, you could go into the provinces at the age of sixteen or seventeen and be an apprentice—not a messenger or "go-for," but a minor participant in the creative process of acting on stage. You didn't go into the provinces to study acting and learn how to act, you went there and you carried spears and washed the props and you did all that stuff. And you helped in a work sense and you observed and eventually they let you go on stage in a little role. Eventually you went up the ladder, learning your craft through active experience. Without that system then, the workshop came into being.

The colleges didn't help earlier, because the conservatory approach only came later. I don't think Juilliard existed. NYU and all of those theatre programs didn't really deal with teaching or training actors. They may have been better at the technical craft, singing and dancing and so forth. But they never really addressed the basic business of acting. So the workshops, especially in the big cities, took over that role, and if one has access to develop one's skills on that level, it's fine to do so. But in the absence of workshops, you have to find pragmatic outlets to try to learn what the craft is all about.

The ideal situation would be to learn through practice and at the same time have the intensity of a workshop, where at least you could begin to get some conscious perspective on what to do and not do, what works. On one hand, the only difference is that some actors who didn't study in workshop don't necessarily know the craft language. They can't verbalize it, but they know their craft as well as others who did workshops, sometimes better. Because some people can talk a good game of acting and use all of the right jargon but can't act. And there are some actors who can act very well and are displaying all the virtues of the craft but lack the ability to verbalize it. So it's not like making a fetish out of so-called training. It's only that if you don't learn acting from practice, you're going to have to learn it through the conscious experiment of going about it, which is what the workshops provide.

A good workshop is supposed to start from the premise of what the craft of acting is about. And you learn through exercises in the beginning. The way Paul Mann approached it, for the whole first thirteen weeks you didn't utter a word. You did exercises. First you did exercises that help you sensitize yourself. You then did those things that cultivate your imagination practically. You began to deal with handling real-life articles—holding this cardboard coffee container, let's say. You did exercises where you start first dealing with a real cup and then ultimately remember the texture of that cup—how it felt, whether it had water in it, whether it had coffee in it, whether the coffee was hot, and all of that in terms of the difference between them. So therefore when you didn't have the cup, you had to simulate holding it. You would be trained to hold it, remembering all of the sensuous elements of it. In the event that you had to, let's say, act out holding a coffee cup that was either warm or hot, you would begin to know even those subtle differences of feeling. The audience might not eventually perceive it, but it would make a difference to you in terms of your belief in whether you were drinking warm or hot coffee. That's just one element of an exercise.

The other thing we'd do were exercises based on observation. We'd go out in the street and observe people. How they walked, how they behaved. You know, physical elements. Observe objects and be able to cultivate your observational faculties, which ultimately is going to come into play when you're going to have to drive or talk about a Cadillac instead of a BMW or whatever.

The first thirteen weeks had nothing to do with acting out a play. It used to be frustrating. I thought we were going to start off doing, maybe, *Waiting for Lefty* or one of the great contemporary plays of the period. But no. You didn't even get a chance to think about that. All you did were basic exercises. Coming in the door with a purpose. Creating your own scene out of your own situation. Which always used to be a mess because, although the scene was suppose to be no more than a minute or two at the most, generally we never even got beyond the opening. You'd walk in the door and that usually would be it, because you were usually stopped. And then before you'd know it, you had spent a half hour talking about what you were doing before you ever did the rest of the scene. You would have to say what you were there for. And then, like everybody else, you could explain the moment better than you had acted it. And the teacher would say, I don't see any of that. I don't see anything reflected when you come through that door. Nothing that expresses anything about what you tell me you're doing. If you then said, But I didn't get that far, he told you it's got to be evident in your first step—when you put your nose through the door, we've got to see something at stake.

Once again the basics. Action, objective, urgency, and so forth. A purpose. And that is a vague sort of concept until you begin to feel it. Which means that unless you properly prepare outside in advance, when you open the door it's not going to reflect what you say you're there for. I tell that to actors and directors even now. I say, Wait a minute, you walk through the door as if the play is going to start after you're inside. But unless you walk on stage already actively involved in the thought of who you are and what you're doing, it's not going to register. And you're going to walk on stage and you're not going to be alive in any way.

So, basically the first stage of my training—almost the first thirteen weeks—was dedicated to getting the sense or feel of things, not just as a concept, but how it feels viscerally. Now there are many other kinds of sensitizing approaches to introduce you to the thought process of moment-to-moment, step-by-step behavior on stage, which finally after all these years in theatre remain the basics, which still work. I mean it's the same old truth that you can never be on stage at any moment without having something vital to be involved in, thought-wise, acting-wise, in exchange with another character or actor. There's no such thing as being out of it. If actors are out of it on stage, are not involved or related to what's going on at the moment, it is because they are into something else that's unrelated. If we ever look toward them, we must feel that they are involved, acting. Sometimes you hear audiences and actors say that somebody is not playing with the other actors, someone is not relating. You, the actor, are focused on somebody and it's obvious they should be listening to you or focused on you, but their thoughts are somewhere else. Let's say they feel that since you have all the lines, they might as well be thinking about their laundry and not thinking about what you're saying despite the fact that they were supposed to have been listening. That's a crime to actors who know their craft. If the scene means for you not to be directly related, then you still have to be actively thinking other thoughts about that situation and so forth. But those thoughts are what all of the exercises, all of the sensitizing, all of the outside observations, all of the physical representations, et cetera, are preparing you to do.

Another example. Maybe you have to mime coming in and picking up invisible clothes. And the difference between the drape of a cloth or the rigidity of some other material, the difference between the feel of paper or the feel of cloth, all of those subtle distinctions eventually mean that the actor's thoughts and tools have to be ultrasensitized. Because what you are going to be dealing with, a lot of times, are invisible things that you have to create with just your imagination. Let's say this glass I'm holding now is supposed to be filled to the top with liquid. But the careless actors get sloppy, they start off with rounded space and next thing you know that hand is closed, which means that they just broke the glass. Or else they forget and then the hand tips over and the water just spilled all over the floor. The irony is, most of the time when the actor is sloppy and does not sustain illusions with exactitude and discipline, the audience knows it. Once you show an audience that you're drinking something and they can see that the glass is almost to the brim and then they see you tip your hand over and forget that you're holding it, especially if you have some kids in the audience, they will probably say out loud, Mama, he just spilled all the water.

So, the initial function of a workshop is to train and prepare you, in various ways, through exercises, to be fully involved imaginatively, creatively, intellectually, and emotionally in the truth of every moment while you're on stage.

THE STANISLAVSKY SYSTEM,
OR METHOD

There's been a lot of talk lately, pro and con, about the Stanislavsky Method. What's your take?

It always came across to me that the origin of the Method was from practical observation. When you read Stanislavsky's books, you find that the foundation was created at a particular time in history. Stanislavsky, in observing acting of different kinds of theatre works, from the romantic plays of the earlier time to opera and larger-than-life genres, began to observe what was effective, how it was effective, and in what way. He had to systematize to a certain extent the best of what was effective with what was succeeding in the romantic period and the romantic plays. Then there was a more realistic style of playwriting from Ibsen and Strindberg and so forth. Suddenly the prevailing modes of the romantic styles of acting just were not sufficient to fit the emerging realism of the art and the effect on the audience of seeing things represented in a more realistic fashion. And out of that observation, et cetera, emerged his systematizing forms, exercises, and analysis of acting as a general mode of urgent communication.

So in my view, the Method was a natural outgrowth in terms of the needs of communication and the necessities of dealing with a new style and a new content. You could not continue with that stylized, almost artificial, French romantic style of acting that prevailed in the Western world. So Stanislavsky came up with certain things that were common to what was good within this transitional period—the function of the actor, those things that made performance work, that made it not work, that made it effective, that made people respond in a particular way, and so forth. In a lot of ways, like any pioneer to a certain extent, he analyzed, made clear, and systematized what was real. Similar to Freud and the Marxists and all those people who were pioneers in suddenly observing and saying, this is the way things are. This is what's underneath the methodology and what's behind it. And what made it clear to us. So his system became a pragmatic approach to acting in a realistic methodological fashion.

When people isolate fragments of his methods into this style and that style and put names and labels to it, I don't know what they're doing. I'm not one to make fractional distinctions, because I don't, to a certain extent, understand all of the definitions that they offer. I see inherent contradictions about the function of an actor being chopped up into these little schools or labels to a large extent.

When I first started acting professionally, in plays like *The Iceman Cometh*, I was coming out of three years of intense acting study with Paul Mann in his approach founded upon Stanislavsky. I was in the *Iceman* cast for almost a year, with actors shifting constantly. New actors would come in, others would leave. It was a large cast, fifteen or twenty actors on stage most of the time, together throughout a four-hour play. And let me tell you, I saw every so-called conscious, unconscious, and no-conscious approach to acting that year. The structure of the play allowed me to observe—there were large stretches of time when you were on stage but you were either supposed to be asleep or in a catatonic state. So it gave you an opportunity to hear and observe what was going on around you while you were still involved in the play. You could be inside the play and observe what was going on next to you and around you. There was the old Irish American actor who played Harry, the owner of the saloon. I think he originally came from Ireland. His so-called style of acting was technically mechanical. He had worked it out that he was looking at you at a slant. His eyes were like twenty degrees away from you, and when his cue or dialogue called for him to turn that twenty degrees and square it, he'd meet your eye by closing that twenty degrees to zero. And if your head was not in the exact place that his eye was supposed to connect with you, I mean if you were one degree off, he was thrown. His calculation of what he did was so precise that he needed you to be right there each time he did it. Not a hair's breadth off, or he was thrown. Another thing is that he had worked out how he should say his lines so technically and mechanically that he could say his dialogue, and in between, under his breath, so the audience couldn't hear him but we on stage could, he would be cursing you out. Saying something nasty if he was angry at you or whatever. And yet, on the surface he was giving the illusion that he was a sweet old Irish barkeeper, the character in the play. Playing with him you could become very cynical, because you would think, Well, the audience doesn't realize that this bastard, this nasty old man, has got a painted smile on his face, and they're accepting his warmth, when as you play with him you know that the shit is not really happening and yet you must respond to him as if it is.

There were other actors whose beats were similarly externally calculated, even if they weren't quite as extreme as he was. But they were also convincing the audience in terms of what they were supposed to be saying and what they were supposed to be giving emotionally. But as an actor, when you played with them, you knew this wasn't real. In playing with actors like that, I came to the conclusion that when actors approach acting that way, their technical choices have to be almost perfect to convincingly communicate the illusion. They don't have any margin for error. Their voice must be perfectly matched to the specifics of communicating what their emotion is supposed to be. The choices must be mathematically selected and they must be right. So it's almost harder for an actor of that type, because if they mess up and are off a little in their calculation or their beats, there is nothing there to rescue them. While an actor who really is involved in playing the scene with real spontaneity and believability at that moment doesn't necessarily have to be exact. The truth of your emotional involvement is so there that it doesn't have to be at the same pitch or peak every night to be convincing. You still are convincingly involved. And that's what the Stanislavsky system, or Method, teaches the actor.

On *The Brownsville Raid* opening night, when I did the Mingo Sanders speech to the General, about being utterly appalled that the Army was going to victimize us black soldiers—that I, a true and objective military man, was so appalled that this was going to happen I simply had to object to it—I remember tears just came streaming down my face, the shock and absolute anger of the betrayal was so great. That's the only night it happened. I played the show for two more months and the tears never came again, but I still followed through with the moment. Some nights the reaction might be angrier. Anger might be the dominant edge. Another night the pathos and the disbelief might dominate. But I didn't have to worry as long as I was playing that scene true to the moment. It didn't matter whether there were tears or whether it was a hot or a cold anger. The emotional result of the moment was the same. But actors who calculate technically, if they don't capture the illusion of what's supposed to be, they have nothing to fall back on. If they get thrown off in their conscious calculations, they're in trouble, because generally they don't have much resource, since they're not really involved in the moment in a way that they can adjust to. Like I said, the actor who when he turned his head to look you square in the eye and you happened to be a hair's breadth out of position, he panicked a little and would almost forget all his lines, because he was so thrown that you weren't exactly where you were supposed to be.

Conversely, I have seen brilliant so-called technical actors work. But their brilliance only comes because they make intelligent choices that are letter-perfect in terms of conveying the illusion of the emotion. The illusion of involvement is convincing. Only those playing with them will know that it's mechanically and technically done, that it's not really truly felt. So you have to make an adjustment when you play with an actor like that. Because if you're really involved and spontaneously believable in what you're playing, you have to adjust to the fact that you're not getting any real feedback. You're getting the illusion of feedback, yet you must respond as if you're getting the real thing. So it puts a burden on you to follow through without getting a comparable exchange on the same plane. You're truly involved, and they're thinking about their laundry list. But they've calculated it so technically that they can promote the illusion of being right character-wise and emotion-wise, and don't need to be truly involved.

For all actors, whether they think consciously about being Method actors, Stanislavsky actors, or technical actors, the bottom-line results are really the same. Despite conscious thought and ideas about technique, it's impossible in the process of a real give-and-take on stage not to have a semblance of real involvement. And actors who go with the feeling and are really involved must still have some technical equipment and must employ some technical means to be involved and to communicate that involvement. Ultimately both approaches lead to the same result. The best actors wind up at the same place, no matter how they get there.

The Work

AUDITIONS

*Over the years of running the NEC and directing so many plays, I
know you've done hundreds and hundreds of auditions. How did you
conduct them and what did you look for?*

Basically, I've had two kinds of auditions. I have auditions for particular plays where I provide as much of the script as possible. I try
to give the actor the whole script to look at even when they're only
there about fifteen minutes to a half hour. I tell them to go ahead
and take the whole script. I tell them what section to look at, the
one I'm going to use for the audition, but then they can also glance
through the rest of the play to get an idea of what the whole thing
is about.

For the second kind of audition I request people to prepare
things in advance. Usually I ask for three different things. A, I want
a scene from black dramatic literature. That's a requirement.
Whatever that is, whatever their choice is. B, they should prepare a
scene or speech with elevated language. Some people would use that
old, tired word *classical,* but I use the term *elevated language,* because
it could be anything, from any source that's not prosaic. It could be
poems or anything that causes the actor to have to tackle language
above or apart from prosaic everyday dialogue. And C, the third
thing, if I have time, is usually something comedic. And all three
pieces should take no more than five to seven minutes all together.
Monologues are fine if that's their choice. And once they do that, I
can get a perspective on their range and to some degree their talent
and command. So, actors when they come in prepared, it's their
choice. It's all theirs.

When I'm reading people for a specific play, then I come in
and give them material according to the amount of time we have

available. I will talk to them about it before and explain whatever needs to be explained. I try always to treat an actor like I always want to be treated. I want actors to be treated with total dignity. And by dignity I don't mean it as an abstract thing. I want you to be relaxed, yes, but I also want you to be as familiar with the material as I am able to let you be under the particular circumstances. I want to give you a shot at doing your best.

My way of dealing with material that is not a monologue, but involves a relationship, is I always read with actors if I can. I'll read all the other characters, so that I'm feeding them knowledgeable dramatic information, giving them the right reading, not have some nonactor or staff member just drone lines at them so they have to provide their own response without any stimulus or motivation. See, I read with them, because I know what the part and the play is all about. I can read with the person, feed them the lines, and at the same time my ear and other antennas are able to judge what I'm hearing.

And what exactly do you find out?

First, I can tell on a limited level how good they are. Whether they are decent actors in general. What would they be right for. What are their qualities. What persona, presence, do they bring apart from whatever the talent quotient is. Then on another level, what is the range of what they can do, is it versatile or narrow. And finally, if it's a specific need, how right are they for the particular play I'm casting.

From the actor I expect an intelligent reading of the material he or she was given, some flexibility in taking the simple directions I've given them, and some demonstration that they are able to listen as well as speak in a dramatic context.

COLD READINGS

Cold readings tend to be one of the most troubling aspects of the audi-
tion process. They can intimidate and sometimes immobilize actors.
When you audition for parts, how do you handle cold readings?

A cold reading, fifteen minutes with a side [a sheet containing the
lines and cues for a single theatrical role/scene], is not ideal, and that's
why when actors reach the stage where they have some status or clout
they ask to be given the whole script overnight. Like I myself would
say, I don't read sides. I will read that side that you need to audition
me with, but I need to see the whole script so I can get some perspective on the character and the material. That's ideal.

   If you have to do a cold reading, my advice is basically just to
try to make sense of what's there. Don't try to act, even though
sometimes the people auditioning you want to force you to do that.
They want you to do some bad acting. I'd rather not do that and
risk not getting the job so I don't get into any bad habits. That
sounds very elegant and maybe elitist, but that's the way I feel.
Now, I know actors who say, damn it, I will do anything to get the
job. But hey, if you've got to be jumping up on the table and beat-
ing your chest or doing some outlandish things, you should want
to know the reasons why. And you are entitled to some reasonable
explanation. All those insane stories, and maybe some of them are
true, about actors in Hollywood jumping on the desks and pro-
ducers saying, oh that's it. Maybe there's some validity to that, but
I have my doubts.

   But what we are talking about is the straight cold reading. My
advice is, if you don't know, you read it to the extent that you know
what's there and what you're capable of doing. And since you haven't
memorized it, you're still reading it. So the trick is to read it slowly,

47

thoughtfully, and well. Now, most of the time you can pretty much guess at ninety percent of what's there anyway by just reading it. You don't have to look for underlying depth. So you read it with sense. You read it with some indication of the situation and your relationship to the character to whom you're talking, even though frequently the other person reading is droning the other part and you've got to provide your own impetus and urgency. But you read what's there according to how your intelligence perceives the situation. And you read it to the degree that you can make sense of it and at least communicate some of the elements of the dramatic situation and the character. That's about it in terms of a cold reading. Once you get a script and are able to read it overnight, you familiarize yourself with it to the extent that you can read it with as much confidence as you can—or, if it's possible, commit some of it to memory. Then you can have more confidence in communicating it.

With a lot of commercial auditions you're not reading with a live person right there, you're reading for the camera. They tape it and send it back to wherever. They come to New York, they tape you, and send it back to the West Coast. They're putting it on tape. So you're addressing yourself to the camera even though somebody, the assistant or whoever, is off camera feeding you the lines. But you make sense out of what's there as much as you can, again with as much confidence as you can about what it is you're saying, and communicating to some degree what the character is all about. You do the best you can and let the chips fall where they may. You have no idea what they have in mind, it's out of your control, so don't let it get to you. My advice to actors is admit to yourself that you want the part but don't need it.

CALLBACKS

What is the reason for callbacks? And what do you want from the actor then?

Basically, when I call actors back, I'm just reducing the previous pool. I'm narrowing the field of possible actors for a particular role. I've made a judgment that these people should be called back. Then always with a callback I tell them a little more about what they're doing or about the character. After telling them sometimes, according to the situation, I will read with them. I will feed them lines in a way to see whether they are flexible enough to respond spontaneously to being directed.

If after I see you the first time, I say, okay, this person is possible, then I'll call you back. Now I will tell you more about the character. Let's say you've got a chance to look at the part overnight and then I read with you and feed you stuff on an even stronger level than before to see how you respond. And let's say you still basically give me the same response that you gave me before you knew what you know now, before you were fed with more authority and so forth. And you still respond no differently than your first reading. Then you might go down in my estimation and possibly eliminate yourself from consideration for the role.

So the thing is for the actor to progress more and be fuller, more authoritative, and more confident than she or he was before. That is what I would say is looked for and expected at a callback.

DISCIPLINE AND INTELLECT

Is there an intellectual process that goes into acting right from the beginning?

Yes, because without that element I'm afraid I am not going to be very compelling or mimetically believable. But I'm talking about something more than that. I'm talking about the moment I'm out there attempting and succeeding in re-creating the essence of, let's say, Adolph Hitler to the point that the result is frightening. The only way I can be frightening in that situation is not so much by commenting on Hitler, but by being Hitler from his own point of view. Without that intellectual exercise, I'm not going to be able to do it very well. And that's the center of being an actor. It is not just some series of spontaneous, instinctive, intuitive reactions. A lot of spontaneity and intuitiveness and so forth ultimately go into it after you have done all of the conscious planning. After that you make it spontaneous. But it's through a consciously willed effort. You must become willfully engaged, and that is where the intellectual process begins.

Let's talk about jazz musicians. All of that flow and ease and spontaneity and improvisational skill of a Charlie Parker and a Miles Davis. Does anyone really think that came just through total spontaneity and intuition or whatever? No. It came through a great effort of conscious practice and calculation and study and more practice till finally I am now free to be spontaneous.

I can tell you, it was only after my fifteenth year of regular professional work as an actor that I finally felt that I truly owned the space. And that I could, with preparation, be free and spontaneous. I was sufficiently in control and had a strong enough grasp of my skills through practice, long practice, that now finally I could fly through a part spontaneously. But that took fifteen years of work and practice and sharpening skill. Honing all of the things I learned that allowed me to be free. So the whole idea—and it's not a unique idea—of spontaneous, creative freedom on stage comes from preparation, discipline, and hard work. Because I have worked so assiduously at my craft, through practice, it now comes easy. This spontaneity that we all aspire to is only arrived at through discipline. Only discipline can lead you to freedom.

Without coming up with a neat definition for the question you asked me, once again, in a fragmented sense, I am returning to the ingredients of what acting is, separate from just behavior that can be exploited. When we were talking about those movie stars, those athletes, those singers, those people off the street who can be used effectively, I said a good movie director can effectively use non-actors, if they can isolate or for the moment capture the real-life behavior of somebody—really capture it. And it works because the script or the moment calls for it. It can work within the set scheme of things. It can be exploited, it can be utilized, and with technology you can then heighten the illusion of its believability, its rightness and correctness, within a certain situation.

However that illusion is harder to even think about trying on stage, and that's why the stage is the realm of a true actor. The stage is the environment and context in which the actor is totally responsible and in charge of the final result. I don't care how many weeks the director works and shapes the performance or the interpretation. In the final act of performance, the actor is totally in charge of what takes place. And there's no one else there to help heighten it or shape it. There are no mistakes to be edited out or anything like that. Therefore the particular mastery of skills and so forth is more demanding. And that's where the actor is on his own and must be in command of all of these skills. Yes, all performances use what actors bring as physical type, presence, and so forth. But on stage, even in the right, realistic type of situation, the actor cannot be effective in the time and space of a stage environment unless his skills are well developed intellectually.

THE ACTOR'S EGO

The ego, as described in various dictionaries, is, A, the part of the psyche that is conscious, controls thought and behavior, and is most in touch with external reality and, B, an exaggerated sense of self-importance, conceit. It is or can be very important to an actor. What does it mean to you in terms of actors and acting?

Actors must be realistic about who they are and how good they are. They must be accurate about that, and if they are correct, they have every right to be egotistical about how good they are. Once you are secure in that, then in truth you will have no ego when you approach the work. Because then you are so good that you are ready to lend yourself to the demands of the work and to fit into it in whatever way necessary.

An actor comes in bringing a strength. Therefore this actor has to have an ego that says, I can hold an audience's attention for two hours or more by myself. And be realistic about it. Because if they're not accurate, they're in trouble. Then they are conceited without evidence. But if you really are true about what you bring in, then you do the opposite. You give in and allow yourself to surrender to direction. You may want to know the reasons why you have to make particular choices. And you should be given the reasons out of respect for your craft, talent, and experience.

I basically never had that problem with actors at the NEC because of the way I work. Everybody always knows what the sum result is. It's not a secret thing. I don't pull actors aside and whisper secrets. No. Everybody knows pretty much when you first sit down what the whole play is about and where it's going. I try to get everyone to understand the interpretive endpoint so that they will accept the choices I ask them to make for their individual characters. Now once actors are secure with that, they still need to know in many instances why the choice is required, and you then remind them, okay, this is the reason for the choice. I'm asking you to make a particular choice here because it fits into the whole picture. The one that you just came up with, right now in the process of rehearsal, doesn't fit, so I'm asking you to abandon it, reshape it, or select a different one that'll fit better into the whole concept.

For me, the actor with a healthy ego is a secure actor. And this is an actor confident enough to subordinate his individual self to the overriding concept of the whole enterprise.

THE ACTOR'S EMOTIONAL TOOLS

What are the emotional tools of the actor?

As far as I am concerned, there is no such thing as an emotional tool. Emotion is not a tool. Emotion is a natural possession we all have as humans. But emotions are not manufactured or generated. You don't play emotions like a musical instrument in order to mechanically get your arms to extend or rise above your head or your vocal chords to vibrate effectively. Emotions are a natural outgrowth of your involvement in a situation. There's nothing that we do in which emotions are not involved. But there's no separate thing called emotions.

Playing emotions is, I guess, what Shakespeare means by tearing a passion to tatters, in *Hamlet*, act 3, scene 2:

> *Speak the speech, I pray you, as I pronounced it to you, trippingly on the tongue. But if you mouth it, as many of our players do, I had as lief the town crier spoke my lines. Nor do not saw the air too much with your hand, thus, but use all gently, for in the very torrent, tempest, and (as I may say) whirlwind of your passion, you must acquire and beget a temperance that may give it smoothness. O, it offends me to the soul to hear a robustious periwig-pated fellow tear a passion to tatters, to very rags, to split the ears of the groundlings, who for the most part are capable of nothing but inexplicable dumb shows and noise. I would have such a fellow whipped for o'erdoing Termagant. It out-herods Herod. Pray you avoid it.*

This great speech regarding what not to do still applies. You don't play emotions. People who play emotions are the worst kind of actors, in that they mechanically milk elements of what we call emotion for sentimental value. Emotions evolve as an outgrowth of what we talked about earlier. You're wanting something and pro-ceeding to act toward gaining what you want, and in the process of it emotions emerge and are naturally stimulated and provoked by your success or failure.

We have needs. We have wants. All of us. That's a given. We want something. We want love. We want power. We want approval. We want to be left alone. We want to be involved with other people. All of these things stem from our desires and our needs and so forth. And the process of achieving them or not achieving them leads to what we call emotional results, or aftermaths. We're encouraged because we've achieved something. We are satisfied, even if it's only momentarily. We are elated by a victory. Or we're disappointed. We get crushed. We are saddened because of a loss. We get destroyed, we say, by defeat. But it is the process of seeking what we need and what we want that led to the emotion. Not abstractly talking about, I'm playing sadness, I'm playing happiness. You don't play happiness. It's an outgrowth of being satisfied by a need or a desire fulfilled. Or just the opposite, you are depressed because of your frustration at not achieving something, being denied, being rejected. Real actors don't sit and talk about, we are now going to practice sadness, we are now going to practice happiness.

Any good director or teacher will tell you, don't try to cry. The worst thing in the world is to try to cry. If it doesn't happen natu-rally out of the process of your involvement or your engagement in trying to achieve something, then it's going to be like actors using glycerin to show that they're crying. I'm referring to the live process. See, you can do that crap making movies. But on stage all that usu-ally happens when you see an actor trying to cry, is you don't believe in what they are supposedly crying about. We reject it because it's like you're milking me. You're playing me cheap. You're insulting my intelligence. You're trying to manipulate me, and that's when the audience rebels. When they see through it. Now as I said earlier, there are some actors who can shrewdly, calculatedly, perform in such a way that they give a reasonable illusion of feeling that some-times the audience accepts. But they've got to be very skillful in order not to be caught. But if it's a real feeling, the audience senses that you're not trying to play the emotion in an isolated way but that it is emerging out of just what we talked about—the frustration of being thwarted in trying to achieve something or being suppressed in your aims, or conversely, being rewarded and fulfilled. Emotion rises out of the action, not ahead of it.

As far as emotional *recall,* I already covered that essentially in talking about the sensitizing of your antennas. And also your observation of life and your involvement in the world. In other words, your grasp of what's going on in life. How broad your emotional possibilities are depends on how broadly and deeply you are engaged in the world, how you address what goes on in life and the world, and how you develop your responses and actions in what I consider to be a humanistic embrace of life. That sensitizes you to identify and be committed to the "positive" aspirations of the human species for survival and to be sensitive to that which contributes to human existence in the most positive way.

That's why Fascism and Nazism do not produce art. Because it is a narrow point of view about human existence. It is a philosophy that champions the destructive control of one set of people over everybody else. That doesn't leave much room for what we call the depth of emotion about anything but selfishness. It's a very inhumane point of view because it's not designed for the greater good of the majority of the people. It's just the opposite. It's for the selfishly narrow satisfaction of the smallest core of people. And that sort of attitude will not allow you much emotion, breadth, or sensitivity to deal with what I call the widest range of human inclusiveness, human existence.

What I'm saying in some ways is, acting is a very humane profession. But this has nothing to do with us being unable to play, to the nth degree, inhumane situations and inhumane characters. Acting by nature is a humane endeavor, because of the breadth of what you are called upon to do. And an inhumane outlook does not equip one to understand or be involved in the widest breadth of human experience.

THE VOICE

We talked about accents before. What about the voice in general as part of the actor's equipment? How important is its development?

Since it is a craft element that is a means to an end, yes, the voice is important. Speech variation is important only in the sense that you have to be able to sound like more than one person. Everybody in real life is quite comfortable speaking the way they do—in one register, or what have you, one tone or sound. But an actor is called upon to represent, interpret, and communicate the whole sum of human behavior. That means everything. Consequently, you have to be trained enough to be able to do that with all the tools at your disposal. You have to have a flexible instrument, vocally. You have to be agile, physically. And all of these things you train, just like athletes. The final goal of an athlete in undertaking all that intense training is to be able to play the game with great agility and, ultimately, to win. You can't play basketball unless you build up your stamina and become elastic and flexible enough to put the ball in the net. Or box without a fast left jab that you're able not to telegraph. Or play football or baseball without the hand-eye coordination to catch the ball and instantly control it, flip it back or throw it forward. All of those things take skill.

It's the same thing with an actor. You develop those physical skills to allow you the broadest range of possibilities. Because you never know what you will be called upon to do. And the voice is a very important part of the whole process. It must be attended to, trained, and developed in such a way that you, the actor, have every confidence in its ability to adapt to any kind of character and any kind of speech or linguistic demands.

THE ACTOR'S EAR

Over and over at auditions and in rehearsals I have heard you use the term "actor's ear," and although I have some general idea of what you mean, I'd love for you to talk about it in specific terms.

Yes, I do often speak about the "actor's ear" or having a "good ear" or a "bad ear." And I'm not always sure people know what it is that I'm talking about. I'll try to explain. In simple terms, I'm talking about how a script sounds to the actor when he reads it dramatically. The ear aspect of it is really the dynamics of sound. It's not comparable to a musician's trained sensitivity to sound, an ear for the very exquisite, sort of minute differences of sound levels, balances, octaves, and all of those technical things. I'm not talking about that. I'm talking about something else.

Generally, actors try to communicate with each other and make sense in what we're saying to each other, to get across a point. In the process of doing that, we use the available means of communication, we put words together into what we call sentences or what have you. We try to communicate a meaning and we do it through, not drama, but through the structure of the language. We emphasize certain things in order to make them more important or less important. We use tones. As black people in particular, we know that it's the tone of communication that sometimes is most important. We use the words *mother fucker* ten different ways, and we know when to fight, to shoot and kill somebody for calling us a mother fucker. We also know when *hey, mother fucker* is meant to be friendly. We know that the tone of it will give us a clue to its meaning.

When I say actors don't have an ear, I mean that some actors can pick up a text that has all of the guidelines writers, particularly good writers, have logically set down regarding meaning and where the emphasis is to be placed and where the stress is to be made and still not communicate it or get the point across. Actors—not all actors, but enough—tend to do everything but that. The reason they don't is because that's too simple, they've overcalculated what their function is; in a funny way, they think acting has nothing to do with communication but has something to do with sound and fury. The tendency for these actors is to pick up a script and read it every other way except the way it was intended.

I used to do an exercise with Elizabeth, my daughter, when she was nine or ten years old. I'd bring her scripts and say, Elizabeth, read this for me, and she would read them with sense. Just like you pick up a newspaper. Now, if sometime you want to do an exercise—I never thought of this, but maybe this would be a good exercise to try with actors—have them read the newspaper. Forget the script. Just have them read the newspaper and see what they do automatically. See if they can read it cold and make sense of what they're reading. Here's an example. I just picked up this newspaper, and the headline says, "Senate Attacks Gay Studies." You could tell me what the Senate did. It attacked. This must be an article about the Senate being against gay studies, so much so that it attacked them. Right? Then, "The Senate voted yesterday to cut off Federal funds to any school district that teaches acceptance of homosexuality as a lifestyle." I just read that, and you know I'm communicating. I made sense. Okay. Why in the world would an actor pick up a script that says this same thing and read it as, "The Senate *voted* yester*day* to cut off *Federal* funds *to* any *school district* that teaches *acceptance* of homosexuality *as* a lifestyle"? It was hard for me even to distort it enough so that it wouldn't make sense. But some actors do it to dialogue all the time. They don't make sense. By the time they finish, I don't know what they said. The audience has not the remotest idea what is being talked about. Dialogue can be a simple, "Hello, how are you?" or "Hel*lo, how* are *you?*" What the hell are you doing vocally going up and down tone-wise, inflection-wise, emphasis-wise in your reading? Why does this happen? Because for some reasons actors think, I must do something with what is there other than what makes sense.

When I talk about a "good ear," I'm talking about starting from the premise that you begin with making sense of the text. Even with a text that is difficult, give somebody with a good ear enough time and they will hear it right even when they don't know it or it's not familiar to them. They will find out, through a few readings, where the sense of it is. And once they start from that simple premise, we can talk about honing it, refining it, and find acting-wise where the sense will always be. According to circumstances and context and everything, it may take on different emotional value or coloration, but never a different sense. And when somebody doesn't have a good ear, they usually do just the opposite.

I've seen it with Shakespeare, when nobody knows where the sense of the thought is, so they think they can do anything. I'm talking about so-called good or classical actors. You get actors playing iambic pentameter and you still don't know what the hell they're talking about. They'll arbitrarily jump, many decibels, a whole octave, with one vocal leap. Without any steps between. I look at the illogic of the fact that they just technically went up two or three decibels without any bridge. The ear of the listener could never understand what they are talking about because it's too abrupt a shift, from here to there without at least a stairstep to slide you over this register to two or three registers higher. Suddenly I'm whispering and then I'm very loud. And you say, what did that fool say?

To clarify my thing about the ear, I'm not talking about a musical ear, I'm simply talking about making sense of what you're reading or saying. That is the foundation of it. Particularly if you're dealing with text. I mean, say I'm attending your theatre and an actor playing a role keels over right there in the middle of the performance and has to be taken away. You need to complete the performance, so you send me on stage and I've never even seen the script. I'm saying you could hand me a cold script. You could give it to me and say, we need you to go out there to finish the performance. And I could deliver a reasonably acceptable performance, just by communicating the straightforward sense of the lines I'm saying.

Anyway, the point I'm trying to make is, when you first start with sense, you can succeed. Because I'm not trying to act first. I'm just trying to make sense of what it is I'm presenting. Now once I find out all of the details, then I can add dimensions to it. But even if I picked up the script cold and gave straight sense to what the dialogue said, it would be at a certain level intelligently effective. "Ear" is really common sense, applying simple common sense first. And this is such a truism: for actors, it is one of the simplest things and yet one of the most difficult concepts to penetrate, precisely because I think most actors feel that in order to justify the function of them being "actors" they have to "act." And therefore they impose unnecessary theatrical stuff on top of things before they even make straightforward sense of them.

The good actor, the actor with the "good ear" will do just the opposite. He or she will make sense of what's on the page in a simple, comprehensible way without trying to load it with an actor's tricks.

SELF-CONSCIOUSNESS AND INHIBITION

What about self-consciousness on stage? What makes it happen, and what should one do about it?

There are a lot of things that make it happen and a lot of things that impede it. We talked already about the frame of mind that you must bring. I mean the seriousness of intent and your purpose to be free and if necessary open yourself to carrying out all the functions that the play requires of you. That being the case, you do everything possible, everything you need to do to carry out the role. And doing those things helps you not to be inhibited.

Being inhibited is to be self-conscious about considerations outside the values of the play. You maybe are thinking about your boyfriend: if I kiss my partner passionately on stage, my boyfriend or husband is in the audience and he's going to be uptight about it and therefore I am self-conscious about doing it because if I do it fully, he's going to wrongfully interpret it as perhaps I'm ready to cheat on him. And if you entertain those thoughts, then of course you are going to be inhibited. This would prevent you from concentrating on the moment. Conversely, the thing that causes you not to be inhibited is concentrating totally on your action and objective within the situation. Once you do that, you will forget entirely that your husband or wife or whoever else is in the audience.

The worst, the very worst, performance I ever gave in my life was one night when suddenly I got ambushed in *A Raisin in the Sun*. I had brought my parents up from Louisiana and put them in a hotel and they went out to dinner and then they were going to see the show. To see me act for the first time professionally. And suddenly, as soon as the show started, instead of being involved in the situation, all that was in my mind was my parents sitting in the middle of the house. All I could do was see these two people sitting in the dark. I couldn't concentrate. I couldn't remember my lines. By the time the first act ended and the other actors realized I was in trouble, people came to comfort me and said, don't worry. And I said, you all are going to have to pull me through. I don't know what happened. I just can't function. It's like I go on stage and instead of seeing you and talking to you in the play, I'm talking to those two people—my parents. That happened quite unexpectedly. I didn't know how or why, and I couldn't figure it out. As I said, I got ambushed. So, okay, this came as a surprise, and once it happened I said, well, I've got to anticipate things like that now. So for the rest of my career I did anticipate when my wife and my children were coming and employed extra effort to concentrate on stage.

I've done plays where I know that my children are going to be absolutely thrown off by the surprise of seeing me do what I am required to do. When they were young, I knew it really was going to shock them. Here they are looking at their father, but they are seeing someone else that's not their father. I had to deal with it. And dealing with it helped me explain to them what acting was all about: yes, it was Daddy up there, and he was doing awful things that's not like him, but this is what acting is. You know, you find a way to explain it.

But you've got to anticipate it. Those are the things that really cause inhibitions or difficulty in concentration even when you have the best intentions about surrendering yourself to your role. So you have to work at it. Because the goal is always the same and your commitment remains the same. And when it happens, you know that your commitment is still to give as much of yourself to the role as is humanly possible. You don't ever surrender that. Concentration is a very fragile thing. You have to work hard at it. Likewise, inhibitions. They just don't vanish on orders. They have to be overcome by strenuous conscious practice.

PLAYING THE ACTION

I guess giving yourself over to a role is what you would call "playing the action."

Yes. As an actor, the action in a role refers to what you want and how you go about getting it. It sounds oversimplified, but finally, if there's any common, universal element that drives a performance, this is it. I don't give a damn what you do, in what style or what form, this is applicable to everything you do. It sounds so simple. It is simple. And that's why it has instructed me as an actor and also as a writer. It instructs me as a director, too. If actors are floundering in any context, at any time, I can always reduce it to basics and say, how are we going to make this scene active? How are we going to make this scene have vitality, vividness, and urgency? Let us find and play the action.

I have never seen a performance work on stage where the actor has no purpose. There's never a moment when you look up on stage and it's dramatic to see that the actor doesn't have any purpose. There's nothing energizing about someone being on stage not doing anything. Not thinking anything. It just doesn't work. Why should I pay to sit in the theatre and watch someone go to sleep without any purpose? Even when you say that the character is bored, every-body knows boredom cannot be played as real boredom. As an actor you must actively play something else that for the audience trans-lates into boredom.

Take your play, *The Offering*. The beginning of the play is what I consider to be one of the most startling, antidramatic, daring moments on stage. A character is sitting there for five minutes doing nothing, absolutely nothing, but watching TV. But, as you remember, the audience was absolutely on the edge of their seats observing his seeming passivity. However, it wasn't that he was doing something extraneous or that he went to sleep. What he was doing was· watching the TV absolutely, to the point of total tunnel-like focus. The action and objective right there was not about him staying awake or falling asleep. It was that he could not be disturbed. He was being attended to by his wife, she was filling his glass without him noticing it, for example. But the intensity of his looking was the action that energized that scene. The audience remained interested because of this focus. He was zeroed in on whatever he was looking at. It was so life-and-death compelling that nothing could distract his attention from it. And even in the second scene, when the others came in, he didn't even acknowledge that they were there in a way that seemed to matter. After ten years you, the visitor, say, "I'm here," and he reacts as if he had just seen you two hours ago. He's totally unaffected by your arrival. He's totally unaffected because his focus, in this instance, his acting action, was glued to that TV. And that is what made the moment energized. At no point was he not being involved or listless. Even if he had gone to sleep, it would have been active. Let's say, imaginatively, that he had been looking at that TV set round the clock, and he was still trying to look at it, but he couldn't help but go to sleep. Then his effort would be that he wasn't trying to go to sleep, he was trying to stay awake.

The bottom line, starting from action and objective, is that you can spend three years dealing with all of the elements surrounding that whole concept, but the nitty-gritty of the whole question of acting still reduces itself to when you walk in the door. There's no way I will ever direct a play or teach acting and somebody can walk in the door and only start acting the second after they get on stage. I will have to find out, or tell you, or get you to deal with why are you coming through this door. You don't come through the door, take one step, and then start a play. You start the play out there. You're coming from somewhere to do something. To get somewhere, for some reason. It's as simple as that. Around that alone you can teach five years of acting. And after twenty or thirty years of acting, the bottom line always returns to that. It penetrates everything you do. Every style of play requires this. It has nothing to do with, oh, that only applies to this naturalist style. No, even if you are dealing with Sam Beckett or other writers that don't seem to discernibly provide you with an apparent, crystal-clear motive or objective. You as an actor have to provide it for yourself. Even when some director or some playwright sort of insists, I want you to come on stage absolutely blank, without having anything to think about or do. You've got to come on totally blank. You don't want anything. That's an intellectual conceit. But an actor has to find a reason for *not* having anything to do, for *not* having any interest. The irony is, you have to then say, okay, I know what they want. They want total blankness. But I have to find a way to motivate myself to come on stage actively with total blankness. You have to find that which will give you an energetic presence. Even boredom, even lassitude must be energized.

This reminds me of a book I just read, called *From Ibsen to Beckett,* by Raymond Williams. A wonderful book. It stimulated me to reread the plays that he was analyzing. It's a very comprehensive coverage. I would recommend it to anyone interested in pursuing this question further. But the point I'm trying to make is, whatever all of the various styles that are represented in the book, Theatre of the Absurd or what have you, it still requires a conscious choice on the part of the actor to make a moment have some sort of energy. Beckett puts people in urns, he puts people in static circumstances and all that. And therefore actors think, to create the illusion, all I have to do is to be boring. But the law is just the opposite. All you're going to do by playing boredom on stage is bore the audience. They don't get the meaning of boredom. If you want to represent boredom, it's got to have a meaning behind it. But if you're going to just be bored, then I as the audience am going to be bored too.

Going back to your play. Supposing in *The Offering,* as still and passive as people may have seen me in that seemingly catatonic state, if I wasn't really looking at that television program and I was just mechanically sitting there, that first five minutes would have been not actively frustrating for an audience waiting for something to happen, it would have been just dead and dumb. But I wasn't just sitting there inactive. I was obviously sitting there involved, looking at the TV screen that was so absorbing that I couldn't move. But it could have been equally effective if I had been internally cogitating. At least they would have felt the aliveness of me thinking something.

There's no way that we could have opened the play, and just sat there with nothing happening, and that would have worked. No. Everything about me was active. I was focused on doing something. I was playing an action. And that's the key to all of it. Playing an action.

Preparing to Play a Role

In General

Tyrone, in
The Offering

Louie, in
Louie and Ophelia

Johnny Williams, in
The River Niger

Sergeant Waters, in
A Soldier's Play

Russell B. Parker, in
Ceremonies in Dark Old Men
(1968)

Russell B. Parker, in
Ceremonies in Dark Old Men
(1985)

IN GENERAL

How do you go about preparing for a role?

When I'm preparing to play a role, the first thing I do is read the script several times to see intellectually, mentally, what is there. What elements of the character are already there that coincide with elements of my own self. What part of me is already like the character or thinks like the character. I mean just in isolation. It's not a question of whether the character is a character I philosophically agree or identify with. No. He may be an individual that is loathsome to me personally. But those elements we have in common that I already know, I don't have to work at. I don't have to think about what I must do to involve myself in accepting what's common. I identify with it in an isolated sense.

Then I begin to explore those elements where philosophically or viscerally my own conscious values differ from those of the character I'm portraying and how am I going to evoke whatever accumulation of mental and other elements I'm going to need to convince myself to become that character. My approach to acting is that it's not enough for me just to represent a character. I must commit myself to thoroughly, ultimately, becoming and identifying with that character till I am that character, both mentally and physically.

TYRONE, IN *The Offering*

Talk to me about how you prepared for specific roles. Let's start with Tyrone, in my play The Offering.

The things I was in touch with in terms of Tyrone had to do with extracting elements of his sensuous nature. I didn't have to go too far to identify with that. Also, with Tyrone, my work was about examining where was he coming from. In some ways the wonderful way you wrote it was that your dialogue wasn't explicitly overt. There was a lot that was implied, and one had to find out what was there and what was being implied. So the search for where he was coming from had to do with his value system. I knew that the values that he possessed on the surface were directly opposite to some of my own life values and life beliefs. And therefore when I began to look at where he was coming from, I had to look at it from his point of view, his alienation.

That was in the text. What was there told me that he was alienated. He was a master thief and showed absolutely not one ounce of regret or self-consciousness about anything being wrong with that. Societally, or what have you. He knew he could get his ass put in jail, and had. He knew the risks, but he had at some point accepted or selected them as his way of life. And had done it so well, so long, so thoroughly, till it was, to him what life was all about. Therefore what I've described intellectually as alienation, to him was not alienation. That's the way the world was and is. That's the state of mind I had to adopt and adapt once I had accepted where he was coming from. His goals, his outlook, and all else. Then I had to cultivate an attitude about it that essentially was his point of view. That said the world's mainstream values and moralities were stupid values and bullshit moralities. And all of it was hypocritical. His shit was real.

70

He was a master thief, and fuck the way the world was structured. It deserved to be approached from his point of view.

Once I discovered that this was his frame of mind, I then had to accept that point of view thoroughly. In order to be him, I had to depict it with complete thoroughness, believability, and conviction. Therefore there was never any choice about anything I did in that play that would ever allow an audience to think that he had any other attitude except that what he was doing was exactly the norm. When he told nasty filthy stories or whatever. Whatever he did was right. Take that story about the sissy and the woman—when the sissy caught him with the woman, and he cut his dick off, and the dick nearly hit his friend, Malcolm, on the head. That story was told with complete matter-of-factness, as if it was the most normal event in the world. The story was vividly brutal, but it was his tone that characterized his attitude. He was just telling this episode like it was the most normal thing in the world.

Now if you asked me, Douglas Turner Ward, are Tyrone's values your values, I'd say, of course not, my values are my values, which is to say, different. But in order to play Tyrone, I had to play the role from his point of view.

What about the details of acting, playing Tyrone in a specific way, for instance?

I didn't particularly focus on the age of the character, although the character was much older than I was when I played him. I let that manifest itself through the text. When you look at the script, you see that his energy and the mental power are still there. What he says, how he relates, his alertness, his command. What you had in that character was obviously a man of overwhelming power and presence. Even if he had sat through that whole play and never moved out of that chair, the probability of that power and energy and presence would be so evident that there was no need to deal with any element of his so-called chronological age. The chronological age didn't affect his functioning until the last moment, when the heart attack killed him. Apparently all along he was still doing pretty well if he could keep a thirty-five-year-old wife, whom he had schooled and brought up, satisfied with what was going on. Then clearly he was mentally and physically capable. It's like I always tell people, what young people don't realize is that unless we elders get real sick, it's like a race, a twenty-yard dash. For twenty yards we elders still can keep up with a twenty-year-old. It's after twenty yards that the youngster starts pulling away from us. And by the time he hits the tape he's got fifty yards on us. But most things in life are really twenty-yard dashes. So give us twenty-yard contests.

Another thing. There are some actors who in playing a role like Tyrone would decide to attach certain personality behavior traits to the character. They might say, he's an old man. I'll make him sly. I'll make him play games like acting pathetic at certain points, just to get his own way. Or something like that. I don't do that ever. Because I don't work that way. I don't impose what I call results of behavior on characters unless it's organic to the text. Actors do those external things usually to get attention. But sometimes it distracts from the main throughline of the play.

I am an actor who as my acting career has developed has stripped away excess. I don't like anything other than what's necessary. I like essence. And as an actor, I try to strip my acting of anything external. It's clean, it's simplified. I am Tyrone. And what Tyrone became and what defined Tyrone is me lending myself to becoming him, which meant that part of him became the truth of me and the truth of me is just what I say and express. I don't need or want to add those external flourishes as things in themselves.

So the approach was clean. The audience could relate to the cleanliness of his throughline. He said what he said when he needed to say it. He did what he did when he needed to do it. When he got to the scene with the Vegas showgirl and she's sitting on his lap, he's running off at the mouth with his stories and so forth. He was florid, talking-wise and everything else. Then finally he got up and danced for five minutes, exposing and adding more elements to the organics of the moment that were excessive. But it was part of the maximum moment. Now why should I be thinking about some other added shit when all things are going to stand out in naked relief when they're necessary. What he said when provoked then took on more power. When he told the character—what's his name, Martin, the young man—"Look, you don't do that in my house. If you're going to talk to this woman like this in my house, you're gonna get the hell out of here." It was very clean, very clear. When he spoke, what he said, when he made his decisions, they came sharp, with no busy context. There was no excess. That's why when he said things, they took on more weight. At the end of the first act, when ordering a swap of the two women, I say, "You stay here. You stay here and we'll go in there," the whole audience was stunned. Especially young people in the audience. He ordered everybody and everybody obeyed him. A man like that, do you think in reality he would be looking for small touches of nonessential behavior and behavioristic patterns? And as you know, the way the whole play was written, by this time he had cut away everything nonessential in his life. All he wanted to do was what he did. He didn't even go outside. He did what he did and he's secreted himself now to the routine of a very Spartan style of life with only basic needs being met.

All this is to say that my intellectual work was done trying to follow through with the text, what the author had there and what was intended. And as you know, you and I never even talked about the theme. We didn't need to sit there and talk, and I didn't need to overintellectualize about it—talking about, now underneath this is really about thus and such. I chose a theme, you never even said that. I always described the final result of the play as that the old man gave everybody a gift. I mean we never talked about this in a conscious way. You may have never even thought about it that way yourself. It's just there. Finally I said, this man dies a great death, but it's like all three people in the play are left able to deal, at least momentarily, with life better than when they came in. That's my interpretation when I describe the gift that he gave. And there had to be some intention in that direction even though he never revealed it in that way.

I believe an actor has to use his intellect. When I use mine, I add the component of being a writer myself. But interpretively I use the advantage of my intellect. When I get up on stage, nobody knows I'm a writer. All they know is what they see and hear. I'm an actor like everybody else. I'm just saying my process is conditioned by other elements. Once you see me up there, you see an actor. When I talk about the cleanliness of my acting, that's an acting choice. I know other actors who go another way, and although I can be fascinated by them, their choice doesn't interest me. I see actors, particularly in the media, who maybe have to do it busily because it's a different outlet. They think it will give their character an identity because they're chewing gum or using a toothpick. I see actors in the media always looking for it, matchsticks or gum chewing or those little quirks of personality that give that character individuality. Only if something is going to be significant would I even look for some shit like that. I prefer to keep things simple, clean and to the point. That was Tyrone.

LOUIE, IN *Louie and Ophelia*

Now let's talk about Louie, in Louie and Ophelia, *which I also wrote.*

Louie is a glorious character in the sense that he is a man whose mind and whose routine has been reduced to the utter simplicity of a few satisfactory determinations. It's almost like he has three or four major things that satisfy him and that he likes. Certain routines and patterns of thought and so forth till it's almost like the opposite of the real Douglas Turner Ward's mental process. But by the same token it can also be very relaxing to be mentally involved with somebody who is so simple, who's reduced his life down to an utter simplicity of interests. So it's like Louie's interests are reduced to basics, not that he had many complex ones in the first fucking place.

To accept that and involve myself in it subtly was very compelling, an interesting challenge. That he could put up with this woman even when she was getting on his nerves. He could put up with her because, well, hey, why not? Life is too short for me to be interested in getting too uptight about it. That is until finally she went too far and then he explodes. Because, hey, there's a boundary past which even the most accepting man won't tolerate. Of course it never was a point that he was accepting her out of weakness. But there came a point where fuck it, I can do my job, go out a couple of times and have my beers. Even though he had to put up with her bullshit, it was within bounds that he could tolerate. As a character, he didn't have any overriding goals. He found out what he was good at, and said, I'm a good cook. I'm making a living at it. What else is there? I don't need to be a big shot.

Just to totally commit oneself to the so-called total limitation of goals is interesting. I say limitation of goals because some would value-judge it by putting it that way. Louie is only limited in goals if you think of it as about the necessity of having overriding bigger goals in life. But once I accepted his point of view, I believed in it. And that he followed through with those values to the nth degree is a marvelous way to live life. So once again we're tackling the script from the character's point of view.

In preparing to play him, I gave him certain external characteristics. I made him a man who dressed quite well. A man who had a certain sense of himself in a particular way. Why? Because that to me was fleshing out the character organically by looking at why a man like that would be of some interest to a younger woman. In this instance, I had to justify this younger woman's interest in him. Once you had that relationship going, there is no way dramatically that the audience was just going to take it on faith, let's say her interest in an unappealing man or one who was plain to the point of sensual disinterest. That would have been asking the audience to take too much for granted. Why would I, sitting in the audience, want to spend two hours watching this play if the two people were not attractive, but just plain Jane or plain John? Saying, oh, isn't that wonderful. Two people who are ugly or sexless are trying to have a relationship together. How cute. By giving both him and her some appeal, it made them equal in their image of themselves. It would've been a mistake to try to emphasize some other element about them without their being sexually attractive. In a way it would have once again put the audience at a distance, and when you look at it, it's a stereotype. A man like Louie was not a stereotype. He had a sense of himself and a sense of his quality taste in music and other things. Everything about him pointed to the fact that he was clean, sharp, if not dapper.

I have been to many neighborhood bars, and I've seen some men come in who were always impressively clean, in their own way. These people's tastes and their manner of dress also came out of the world they related to. Whether it related to going to the track or to a club. These people had a sense of self and were quite proud about the fact that they were whoever they are.

To not have been true to that vision, that would have made an inorganic comment that I wasn't Louie. It would have been foolish for me to go against that. I'm saying I would have made a point to dress him against my own sensibility of taste and that would be absurd. If I'm going to be him, I would have to try to do everything I could to maximize my getting laid. Anything less than that would have been asking for defeat. And I remember the script never said anything indicating that he wasn't successful in terms of getting intimate with women. Louie basically set the parameters of his own goals and I made him a playing partner. There was not anything in his manner, the way he dressed, what he liked to drink and the music he liked to listen to, that said Louie wasn't aware of who he was. Louie had a good sense of self. A strong sense of self.

Again, we're talking about a certain kind of surrender when you approach a character. It's really a combination. You have to surrender to it, and then you have to use yourself in such a way that makes you believe that you are it.

JOHNNY WILLIAMS, IN *The River Niger*

What about Johnny Williams, in The River Niger?

Johnny Williams is an actor's dream, because he encompasses such a broad spectrum of harmonious and contradictory elements. Johnny is a man of great intelligence, and that's something people don't get immediately because of his gruff exterior. Johnny is not just an intelligent man, he is also a very educated man. He's very aware and intelligent. I mean, the conversations he has with the doctor, their wit and repartee, are of a very cultivated kind. It can be sarcastic and cynical but it is very educated and aware. So, despite his exterior, he is a very sophisticated man in terms of ideas, thoughts, knowledge, and all that. And then he has all the basic qualities of a man's man. You know, I can stand at a bar and drink everybody else under the table. And can be comfortable in any environment. He's profane and gruff and all, but deep down underneath he's enormously sensitive.

Once again you're looking for what you have in common and don't have in common with the character. Johnny Williams is very easy for me to identify with. Because a lot of the breadth of his comfortability in all worlds is me. There is a natural progression of how my own personal history was very much like Johnny Williams. I've always remained true and proud of my class background. I consider myself peasant working class in my origin and fiercely proud of it, but at the same time equally proud of a sophisticated intellectual existence that goes along with that.

Because of his broad, big embrace of all these components, it was natural for me to play him. But for other actors to do him, the director must first get them reaching into themselves to find out what is within them that can match the depth of Johnny Williams' embrace of all these things. It's not easy. Even when I directed other actors, I got elements of his scope, but I didn't get an equal coexistence of all of these elements simultaneously. Some would be better at one thing and less at another. Some would be better at communicating the common-man element of a dude who could bend elbows in a neighborhood bar with everybody and have the fun, revelry, and friendship with his peers and other people in a full way. But a lot of actors could not necessarily grasp and communicate the intellectual breadth of the man. Therefore when they would get to delivering the poem, they would say the poem, but it would be theatrical and it wouldn't be quite believable in the real sense that Williams could have written that poem. And so I would get different emphasis and balance from them.

But the one thing that I could never get to the same extent from the actors is the vulnerability of Johnny Williams. See, the final key to Johnny Williams is this great sensitivity that he covers up with all his profanity and rough surface. But underneath it, the key to Johnny Williams is when he learns that his wife has cancer and curses out God. That is the key defining moment for him. And the interesting thing is with all due respect to all of the actors who played it and played it well, they always wanted to skip over that moment, because it was too revealing. That's the moment when he falls on his knees and says, "Why do you keep fucking with me," when he addresses God. That finally is one of the greatest, one of the most gripping moments in contemporary theatre. Not just because of the scene's emotional content. But because of his helplessness. Finally he has to show it, his helpless passion and fragile vulnerability. He has to let it go really—I love this woman so deeply and I am so stoic in accepting all the shit you put on me but now why this last straw? "Why do you keep fucking with me?"

But actors often want to skip over the moment and get back on their feet, embarrassed to display naked vulnerability. Directing it, I find that you can't tell actors, look, stay down five more beats on your knees. It's too mechanical. If you can't do it, I have to accept how much you can do that's believable. I can't ask you to go any further. Because those are moments, if the actor isn't involved to the point of total emotional exhaustion, then there's nothing I can do. You can't ask the actor to mechanically do something like that. You accept what you get. And if they can't do more, you have to accept the truth of how much they can do and let it go at that. But I know dramatically that many times it has not been necessarily fulfilled totally like it should be.

So the key to that character is his vulnerability. Generally you say, hey, if it's not there, you can't play it, because it's not indicated in the text. But the one element that you don't necessarily find in the text in an overt way is the extreme clue to vulnerability. And that's important, because in *Niger* it finally explains the ultimate capability of sacrifice that Johnny had covered up with his overt talk and profaneness. That's where the urgency of his character lies, to cover the vulnerability. He's always covering up his vulnerability. He's really a softy. But he covers it up with rough talk. And that gives the actor something to work with throughout the play.

You see, vulnerability is something that you have to surrender to in yourself. If it's not there, then you're not going to do it. It's what the actor brings to it. Sometimes if it's not there, it will seem like it's there because the text is so strong, but it's up to the actor to give it the dimension of potential greatness. You could indicate it acceptably, certainly. But it will only be great to the extent that you have it in you and are able to surrender to it. A lot of people just don't have those vulnerabilities in them, especially actors. They should, but they don't. The urgency in Johnny Williams is actually his need to support his family in whatever way possible. He had all these people to carry. This is what he's done all his life. He's sacrificed his own ambitions for the needs of other people.

The poem is a revelation in a bigger-than-life sense of his dimensions. The poem metaphorically sums him up in a larger sense by creating a metaphoric image and then attaching it to a larger framework. A feeling metaphorically about a bigger world, a larger river. But Johnny Williams is, in emotional breadth and scope, the biggest of all those characters.

SERGEANT WATERS, IN *A Soldier's Play*

What was it like to play Sergeant Waters?

I wound up playing Sergeant Waters, in *A Soldier's Play*, after I had directed many other actors in the part. The thing with Waters is, you look at the text closely and you look at my physical and vocal equipment and also the work I had already done in other roles and you say, hey, he could play Waters in his sleep. Without even thinking about it. I could put on a uniform and I'm Waters. All I've got to do is adopt a military point of view. Other than that, everything that existed in the play I could do. Yet Waters basically didn't interest me. In the sum total of all the things I had done, there was nothing that I could add to Waters that would be of any challenge to me as an actor. All I had to do with Waters, once I learned the lines, was commit myself to what he said and did in the text, that's all. There was nothing to explore being Waters, for me.

Waters postdated other roles that *had* interested me. But you've got to know what you've already done. I'd already done Waters in one way or another. In Sanders, of *The Brownsville Raid*, there were many similar elements. He didn't have Waters' contradictions and complexities, but the soldier's component and the thrust of it were similar enough. About his contradictions, in one way or another I had played something similar. So, since I had already done similar characters, acting-wise there was nothing for me to do to be Waters but involve myself in the role.

It was more interesting to me to fit Waters to the persona of all the other actors who played it. And they brought different things. Just think of Adolph Caesar and Graham Brown. Everything about Adolph Caesar was right for the thrust of Waters. Part of Caesar's whole persona was he was always proving the fact that he was a big cat. Caesar was physically small, but that combative pugnacity gave him an interesting quality that was just right for Waters. There are many things in the role that are not commonplace or conventionally apparent. Caesar was the role, but it took a nonconventional perspective and perception of how right he was to cast him in it. Which is what I did.

As I've always said, the more conventional thing would be to cast somebody like me in the role. An obviously big, physically imposing sergeant type, where it was obvious that in his relationship with the men it looked like he could kick their ass or with a flick of his hand control them through his physical presence. That was the expected choice rather than a little five-foot-five, light-skinned, colored dude, despite his big voice. You wouldn't automatically accept the fact that he had that natural control over his subordinates. He had to actively do something to convince them about his authority, and that was much more interesting than the automatic acceptance of a stereotypical DI sergeant type.

The urgency for any actor playing that role is the urgency of not letting these men act like niggers. That's the common thread. That's the throughline of his character. That applies to everyone. You just take different aspects of who the actors are. I come in and the men stop right away, on the dot. Caesar comes in and you might get a sense that they might hesitate a beat, and if he's not looking at them they might not come to attention. They might not accept his authority right off. He might have to look at them twice.

Graham Brown comes in, and Graham on one level would be like Caesar. But on another level, Graham's surface polish might make the men think that maybe he's not the typical sergeant. That maybe he's got more pull with the white people cause he looks more like he's a smooth type. He looks more like he should be an officer with the white people because he's got that sort of sophistication. Once again that might be an element for them to deal with. He is ultimately going to have to deal with the same throughline— he's not gonna let the men act like niggers. We might even expect more of him in his not wanting that because he wants to be more like the whites. It wasn't that Caesar wanted to act like whites, and it wouldn't be like I wanted to act like whites either. Caesar, as the character, is just crazy and obsessed about black folks not being niggers. Graham might make it more logical by saying he wants the black men to act like whites, because he's more like whites himself.

None of these traits or comparisons you read into it would be invalid. Because it is not going to disturb the core of what I said. The commonality is, all of the sergeants are not going to let these men act like what they assume to be nigger, because whenever Waters gets to the final speech that's what it's going to be about. About when he killed that boy in the war. Because that sergeant for the rest of his life said, no, he's not going to ever let his men act like niggers after seeing that black man act like a monkey.

Another interesting thing about *A Soldier's Play* is, in playing Waters, you've got to contrast him to CJ. CJ is who you have to play off of Waters. Waters' anger at CJ is because CJ is very much like Louie from *Louie and Ophelia,* in his own way. He just comes from a more peasant country background. And the white people mean so little to him that even when he grins at them he really doesn't give a damn about them and is not interested in being in their company. He just gives them what the hell they need in order to get rid of them. Get them out of his life. He is the freest person in the play, because he's accepted what he is, and he drives Waters out of his mind, because Waters is one of those blacks who feel you can never let your vigilance down. You can never relax. You've got to always be vigilant about being black and never let yourself be thought of as less than anybody else. It's a vigilant attitude that is taken to its ultimate extreme when you see what Waters does. CJ is just the opposite. So I say you play off of him.

An actor must understand the distinction between these two attitudes and value systems. As a director, you've got to do what I just said. You have to convince CJ that he is free, that the purported limitation in CJ's mind is a freedom of a kind that is to be embraced. And with Waters you have to convince the actor that he has been driven to the point of being ever alert about blackness. Being the mounted police in assuring the purity of black behavior. Now we know that both of these attitudes exist in real life, and it doesn't take too much of an actor's intellectual will to find models if you don't understand it. But all of these things actors must do, in order to interpret these characters.

The repertory of black or African American theatre literature is full of great and interesting characters. Characters that challenge and extend the black actor if he puts his mind to it, and makes an honest effort at creating something that is culturally real. Clearly, we have the plays. The problem is, they don't get done as often as they should. Even our own actors don't demand to play these roles. So they wind up attempting stuff that's far away from them. And generally they do it without much distinction.

RUSSELL B. PARKER, IN
Ceremonies in Dark Old Men (1968)

What about the first time you played Russell Parker?

Well, right away, just on a limited level, right at the beginning of the play, the script tells you that this man is looking for somebody and that it is very urgent that the person get there within a period of time. He's already dealing with time. So on a basic level you say there's something very important that this man keeps looking out the barbershop window for. Right away, before you even know what it is, you know that there is something very urgent, somebody very urgent, that you're looking for. So that's number one.

That means that I've got to start with somebody who is not relaxed, somebody who does not have too much time. The urgency, that for whatever reason I want somebody to get here as fast as possible because somebody else may be involved, but that's all I know. Soon it turns out that it's his buddy. Soon as the door opens and his first line is, "Where have you been," I know already that "Where have you been?" is not casual like, hey, man, where have you been? Right away, I know damn well that it's not casual. It is already told to me before the other person got there that he went to the door, he came back, he sat down in the barberchair and tried to read the paper, and he couldn't even read the paper because before he could, he's looking out the window again. Then right after he says "Where have you been," Parker's buddy says casually that he doesn't feel late. He says he's been at work or whatever, and then Parker even ignores his answer and almost begins to curse him out. He says, "You know what's going to happen if my daughter comes in and finds us playing checkers." So all this urgency you find out right away is about him waiting for his friend to play a game, to play checkers. And it turns out that he wants to get in the game because this time he figures, I'm going to beat you. It's almost like he stayed up all night thinking, I'm going to win, I'm going to beat you. I mean, it's obvious that he wins very seldom. It's urgent for him to play the game, to get the game in before his daughter arrives. So right away you have basic action, objective, and everything else. We don't know the big issue yet, but we know the instant moment.

The basic ABCs of any acting are precisely what I just said. Every moment in a play is on that level. In this instance, it's overtly presented. In other instances, it might be underneath. There might be another play where it's just the opposite, where you come in and say casually to your girlfriend or your boyfriend, "Where have you been," and you say it casually, but it turns out that underneath you are forcing yourself to say it casually to not show that you are angry about it. In one instance it's urgent on top, and in the other it's urgent underneath. They both illustrate the same principle of urgency. No actor can do anything that's unurgent, and ironically no writer should write anything that doesn't have an underlying urgency to it, otherwise why should we call it being involved in drama, which by nature is asking us to believe that when you sit down here, I have something very important and urgent to say to you through this media. This is what theatre and acting is all about.

Here I'm talking about this matter of urgency in stages. And what it reveals to us. There were stages in what you could deal with just on their own terms. Just in both of these instances. Beyond that it goes to a larger thing. We find out eventually the nature of the relationship that he has towards his daughter and why he doesn't want to be caught by her, because he's going to be pushed into doing something he's afraid to do. She keeps pushing him to get a job for the fiftieth time. It's not that he doesn't want to get a job, but he's fearful to look for one because he already knows the result. And once he goes and gets rejected or doesn't find a job, it's going to make him more depressed about dealing with the reality of being a washed-up dancer. So there is a bigger reason why with Parker, and it just keeps expanding, for everybody.

Everyone in that play has very urgent objectives and desires and goals, and they clash in various ways. The older son is anxious about proving his own worth in the world by doing something that he can consider to be an achievement. The younger boy is eager to prove that he's not dumb. He wants to find a way to make his own niche. He does so as a thief. The daughter and the friend have their own urgencies, too. They are sufficiently inherent to the play that you hope the actors will see this by themselves, but if they don't this is what they must be brought to see in order to make the valid interpretation of the material.

So there are the elements that cause an actor to find a clarity in making choices—interpretive choices that will help him or her attack a role. To not do this from these viewpoints will handicap the actor. Let's say the actors must try to figure out, wrong or right, what the actions and objectives are. Because at least that will equip them to make a concrete choice. And even if they make a wrong choice, they will do something concretely enough that at least will show their ability to carry out an interpretive goal. For instance, I will audition actors and they will be totally wrong in terms of the interpretation they made, but they did very well in what they chose to do. And I say, you're wrong, but you showed me. They say, well, can I do it again? I say, I don't need you to do it again; you proved to me what you can do once you were given the right choice. You did make a choice and you carried that choice out right. It just happened to be the opposite of what was required. But you've proven to me that you can act that interpretation. That is what's involved. And they say, oh, I didn't know that. And I say, I know, that's why I'm not blaming you for not necessarily making the right choice. If an actor can do a sensible initial reading of the script and then make a choice close to it all, he or she is well on the way to making a strong and very favorable impression at the audition.

Parker in *Ceremonies* was an interesting and challenging character to play, because there was so much on the surface that the author provided. But there was a lot underneath also. But what we're talking about is the beginning stages in attempting to interpret a character. The other stuff, the underneath, comes during the rehearsal process. But here I'm just talking about finding a starting point.

RUSSELL B. PARKER, IN
Ceremonies in Dark Old Men (1985)

You played Parker again seventeen years later, in the revival. What was that like?

It was interesting. Interpretively I didn't have to do anything, because my interpretation was right from the beginning. The only thing to deal with seventeen years later was, I was now more properly the age of the character, so the weight that I brought to it was the natural weight of my own natural persona. In 1968, when at age thirty-five I was too young, I had to intellectually add weight to it in a preparatory way, as if I was the character twenty years older. But seventeen years later I didn't have to think *as if* I was the age of the character. I was not being the character, I was the character. The character was my twin in every way. Before when I was too young to play it, I had to willfully act as if I were older.

Then too, the play was now taking place in a different time and space, where attitudes and situations had shifted and changed and so forth. The play was being done in a different context, and therefore how it was being reacted to took on the particularities of its own time period. That was different from before. I mean, seventeen years earlier the whole element about those three men not working had no extra edge to it. It was accepted as a common social fact that they were not responsible for and had no complicity about it. It was accepted by the audience, male, female, black audience, that their plight was a norm that was not their fault. And therefore it had no edge to it and therefore some elements of it could be relaxedly looked upon and you could even see ironies and humor about it. Suddenly, seventeen years later, with the whole element of black work and black males being attacked and being viewed almost

88

as if their not doing shit work or ordinary nonrewarding work was their own fault.

So suddenly with the whole question of Parker and his sons, there was a different complexion to it, even more conditioned by a consciousness on the part of the audience that a black woman was taking care of all these men. Seventeen years earlier that was not looked upon with much judgment. I mean, everybody understood the burden placed on her. But they didn't much take her frustration with the men as being something organically wrong with the men. They saw that she was just trapped in something that the men had no control over themselves. Seventeen years later that whole element had taken on a different edge. I mean the black woman taking care of the black men had suddenly, within the black culture, become a more controversial issue. And those elements began to shape the audience response to the play. So awareness of this had to enter into my thinking about the role, both as an actor and as a director. The development and interpretation was more or less the same, but a new element that had nothing to do with the play when it was written entered into the mix. And it had to be dealt with. This was done through certain shifts in emphasis and stronger intensification of certain other elements.

So I guess what I'm saying is that there are always other elements to consider when one reinterprets a role that one has played before. The age factor, the shift in social values, and so forth. You can never just act out of memory. It always comes out of the present and the new circumstances you're surrounded by. Drama is always about change. It's always inside the play, but sometimes it's outside as well.

Critics, Audience, Etc.

Actors and Criticism

*Dealing with the
Audience/Learning
from the Audience*

Sustaining Long Runs

Drugs and Alcohol

Acting in Commercials

ACTORS AND CRITICISM

The critics are always having their say as part of a career whose end result is public performance. What are your thoughts?

Being criticized is part of the process. It is natural in theatre. It's the nature of the profession, and nobody is immune to it. Actors are putting *themselves* on the line and are therefore more vulnerable and more thin-skinned. Even with us as writers, it's almost like a part of us is separate from the work. We say, well, so and so didn't like my writing, but I'm still me. They didn't talk about me personally; they just talked about an outgrowth, my writing. But the only thing actors get put down for is the self. So of course they are more vulnerable and more subject to being affected by and sensitive about it. You're naked up there; part of the work is using yourself. Therefore the likelihood is that given enough time, you're going to have some nasty things said about you. You have to learn how to respond to that.

Generally you ignore it, try not to take it personally. It's also natural for you to want to kick somebody's ass or curse them out. It's natural to say, to hell with them. And for part of you to be furious about it, even depressed, go out and get drunk. That's when the objective part of you has to go over, retrace, rerun in your mind, what your performance was against what was said about it, just to test to see whether there is possibly any spontaneous revelation that can enlighten you to something that could be improved. It's like I always tell actors, even directors or what have you, when they think a review is unfair. I say, get mad, want to fight, do whatever else, and then go home—you never have to admit it—but go home and review what was said to see whether there was one iota of truth about the critique, some observation that might be useful to you for improving your craft. Something weak or something that suddenly is enlightening to you about what was perhaps not achieved. You can use a negative remark and turn it into a positive thing.

But criticism is inevitable for all of us, even for some about whom critics don't know what to say except that they are just as excellent as they always are. But for everybody at some point, somebody is going to cut you into little pieces, and you've got to be prepared to deal with that. Both to figure out whether there's any truth to it, and conversely when you come to the conclusion that there's no truth to it. There are so many reasons people are negative about an actor's work, and many times what they reveal is that they're negative because they're being subjective. This unfairness comes from unexpected places. There was a period when many of our black so-called critics in early days eliminated themselves from serious consideration because of their subjectivity. Their criticism made no sense. You read it or heard it and said, there's something personal about this which doesn't make sense. Yes, of course, nobody's immune, but you have to be tough-skinned.

Getting to me personally. Putting myself on the line in all of these disciplines, sometimes as writer, actor, and director, often in the same play, there were people who got very angry at me for having that much chutzpa and overwhelming arrogance, to dare to be all of these things. You could sense sometimes that when they judged me, that's what they were responding to. It had nothing to do with what I had accomplished in whatever my areas of responsibility. That didn't matter, they just wanted to say, don't do it. Let's put this man in his place—how dare he? This is not past times, this is not the old days when it was legitimate to combine all these disciplines together and no one thought anything of it. Nowadays you've got to be restricted to special categories. A Renaissance man? Who is this fool to think he can do all this?

So you read it, you think about it, look for value in the critique. If it's there, you respond positively. If it isn't, you dismiss it and move on.

DEALING WITH THE AUDIENCE/
LEARNING FROM THE AUDIENCE

What's an actor's relationship to the audience?

An audience is a live organism. An actor is not acting in a cocoon. That's the whole distinction between theatre and film or TV. It's a live process. And an actor can learn from the response he's getting and sometimes calculate what that response should be. I mean, here's where the audience should laugh; here's where they should be upset. That sort of thing. It's most obvious when we talk about comedy. Oh, we know the audience gave us a laugh, so everything is great. That's a literal response to it. Or the audience cried, that's another clue. But that's the most superficial aspect of it, because the audience, even in silence, even in attentiveness or lack of attention, can tell you something about what you're doing or what they brought that affects what you're doing.

Suppose you're dealing with a theatre party, where everybody's been together, they know each other, they may have been to dinner together prior to the show, and so forth. Sometimes the last thing in their minds is the ability to come to the theatre and concentrate on what's up on stage. It may take a whole half a show before you can get them to concentrate on anything. That's just the reality of things, and one has to understand that.

The audience is not an unvaried mass. They're all different. Different kinds of audience. The audience brings themselves, and they can reveal themselves to you. They can tell you in various ways what you're doing in both a positive and negative way. And as far as the black audience, which is my favorite, goes, they are so spontaneously responsive, overt and explicit in their response, they can help you shape your craft. Because dealing with them affects your craft, your timing, your command. They affect how you control and sometimes hold their attention. It becomes your job to change your prior calculation to fit the circumstance as long as it's reasonable. It's unreasonable if the group comes in drunk, you then get the ushers to come and throw them out or what have you. It's almost like the court rule, *beyond a reasonable doubt.* An audience must cooperate enough to give us a reasonable chance at performing for them. But after they give us a reasonable chance, then everything else is up to us. To hold their attention, to keep their attention, to respond to their coughs, et cetera. To not let whatever their natural spontaneous response is throw us.

There are times when very important things are being said in a play and somebody gets something stuck in their throat. You can't ask them not to have something stuck in their throat. It's a living, spontaneous moment. They have no control over it. But they might have to try to get that thing out of their throat just when you're about to deliver your most important line. When you hear that, and your ear tells you that sudden uncontrolled sound will drown out the most important line that you have in the whole play, then you're going to have to repeat that line. Nobody else heard it, because suddenly that cough blocked the line out for everyone. It just takes one cough and the whole house didn't hear that line. So you have to make a decision right there, spontaneously, without missing a beat or getting out of character, that you've got to repeat that line. And it's up to you to come up with some extra energy and some extra involvement to do that. Just like you have to reach for extra energy internally when you're sick. Or when something has happened in your personal life and your concentration is more difficult. You have to, through an act of will, make sure these unexpected circumstances don't seriously affect how you perform.

I mean, suppose something just happened to me about an hour before I got on the subway to come to the theatre. Something in my personal life, my family or something like that. Tonight the last thing I want to do is act. But I have to do the show. How am I going to do it? You're going to find that you've got to consciously concentrate harder to keep yourself involved and keep your thoughts from straying back to your personal problems. Or suppose I've lost my voice. I only have one tone left. How am I going to get through the show? What am I going to do? I'm going to have to concentrate and realize that every time my ordinary voice goes from low to high, I lose it. That means I have to stay away from my high register and still sound natural. I have to stay in my middle register totally. I can't go into my high register because it's going to squeak, I'm going to lose my voice. So I will consciously work out a way to do it technically and still project natural involvement.

You always have to deal with the audience. Sometimes an audience feeds you, and their energy puts you on a high. You're rolling with them because of the stimulus they give you. And that's what makes live theatre wonderful, because you can't calculate it. But you've got to be prepared to be spontaneous and respond spontaneously to what's being given. Audiences shift. Sometimes cold rainy nights put audiences in a different mood and frame of mind. Sometimes those who trudge through the snow are so self-congratulatory of their heroic ability to get there, it makes them a great audience. The fact that everybody else didn't make it but they did, suddenly they are ready to settle in and have a great time. And sometimes when there's only five in attendance, we actors will often strive to give them a better performance than when we have a full house. Someone says, well, are we going to cancel the show, and I say, no, there are five people out there who came through fifteen inches of snow drifts and they finally got here. I say, they got here and they deserve a show. More than just a show, they deserve to see a great show. And we play better for five people than for five hundred. That's how I feel about the audience, and that's my advice on how to respond to them.

SUSTAINING LONG RUNS

How do you keep a part fresh during a long run?

To me an ideal run is anything between four and six months. Anything beyond that and you're in trouble. Between four and six months in almost any great role or great play, you virtually exhaust your discovery. Over that period of time you're getting deeper and deeper into playing the role, and it becomes second nature and so forth. And you wear it like it's your own skin after a while. That process can be rewarding and creative and innovative and all of that. After that there's nothing more to discover by my calculation. Now you're going to have to start using will, guile, and craft to keep the work fresh in order to play it as if you're doing it for the first time. You've got to employ conscious strategies.

Every actor has to find his own way. For me, I find that going back to the script can help sustain me for a productive next stage. During the initial stage, since I'm performing every night, my concentration is fine, so all I need do is to go over the elements of the script in my mind and I'm prepared. But after six months, when suddenly I'm exhausted and bored, then I will take the text and say, okay, let me read the whole script all over again. And just the physical act of going back to the script can shore up my integrity about keeping the work fresh. Because what I'm saying willfully is that I need to keep this fresh. And I know that if I just take it for granted, then I'm tempted to just imitate what I've been doing rather than keeping it new. I know I have to do something.

Going over the script will perhaps show you some new aspects to the story being told and the character you're playing that you never noticed before. This is particularly true at this time because now you've had many audiences functioning as witness/collaborators. Their responses can alert you to other aspects of the work that may have been hidden from you before. So the challenge now becomes one of incorporating those new insights into how you shape and perform the role. Working this way, you can keep a long-run performance fresh. Just the physical act of going back to the script can help you refocus on the need to be honest.

After this, you use all kinds of other imaginative strategies. Consciously thinking about the audience and reminding yourself of the reality that everybody out there is seeing the performance for the first time. You can motivate yourself by saying, I may have done it for six months, but they are seeing it for the first time. And my duty and responsibility to them creatively is to do it with the same involvement and the same spontaneity that I did on opening night. And then—I always laugh about it—you engage in your personal subjective exercises, projections, convincing fantasies, and anything else that will work.

Actors who want commercial careers start imagining that every night an agent is out there in the fifth row. My stimulus probably would be something more profane or more sensual. That maybe out there tonight, sitting in the back of the house, I can't even see her, but it's gonna be the greatest gift of female offerings that I will ever receive in my life. I say, hell, use whatever motivates you to go out there and keep it fresh. Strategies to get you in the frame of mind. To force you to approach the work from a fresh perspective. And all of this will carry you for a while longer.

Eventually, nothing will work, and if you still need the money and can't quit, you know you will be going through the motions.

DRUGS AND ALCOHOL

Drugs and alcohol are common temptations in the performing life. What is your experience in that regard?

They weren't a great concern to me. All I'm saying is that it didn't happen very often with my company, because I had already set parameters and standards where certain practices were just not accepted. Generally, once the actors were hired, I don't remember having too much of a problem. But once you were dealing with shows running, then there were occasional individual incidents. Drug shit that would at times flare up to a point finally affecting performances. In many instances, I was just on the verge of dealing with it when it would cease, or it would never escalate to the point where I would have to deal with it. But generally, it wasn't too much of a problem.

Except, I remember with one show I almost wanted to choke a particular group of actors, they were messing up so badly. And while giving notes I was almost in tears cursing them out. I was lashing into them so viciously, so sharply, till I was crying, but I was still cursing them out. What happened is they had gone beyond the pale, and it began to affect the work. This was during rehearsal before the show opened. It began to have a growing effect. It's like, I was only able to get a half day's work out of them. Because on breaks they would go—at that time it was before the coke shit, this was just pot—they would go and smoke and come back. And you know, if you mess around with pot, there ain't no urgency. Nothing is urgent. With pot, and drugs, you can't act. All the urgency and action and objective I've been talking about goes out the window.

Can you imagine trying to act with urgency on pot or liquor? Yes, liquor has the same effect. It fuzzies up your ability to concentrate. Pot absolutely fucks with your time sense. Anybody who smokes pot knows this. It may affect people in individually different ways, but the payoff is about the same. I know when I've smoked pot, a fire could be happening in the room and all you do is get fascinated by the flame. You just watch the flames until finally somebody in the room might just get up the energy to say fire. And then it takes five more minutes just to get up out of the chair to leave. But you could be burnt up before you can manage that. Due to your impaired sense of time, nothing is urgent. It's not important.

I knew that pot wasn't for me when I found myself on a date in such a state of lassitude that it interfered with my urgent desire to have sex, I didn't need it. It's like, why put out the effort or energy. I feel so mellow. I don't want to have sex, that takes too much energy. That's when I knew it was no good for me, when I said, I don't need this drug.

Anything that interferes with an actor's ability to do his job fully and powerfully should be avoided. It's really as simple as that.

ACTING IN COMMERCIALS

You've talked about theatre, creating a character and sustaining levels of concentration and urgency for extended periods of time. What about short-term acting in the media? I'm talking about selling products, that sort of thing. How should the actor, the serious actor, approach it?

You're talking about acting in ads or commercials on TV. My sense is that the lines have gotten even more blurred than they were before. I think that's because in our modern media world, people think that certain media functions are equal to acting, interpretive acting. Doing ads, creating a career doing one type of thing and getting rewarded for it. You don't have to do anything else. You can play your own persona or take your public image and translate it into something recognizable, like athletes do. The audience responds to you because they recognize you as Michael Jordan. They relate to you just like they relate to a performer playing Michael Jordan or doing a take-off on Michael Jordan or an imitation of Michael Jordan in a stereotypical way. And all of these things get thought of as acting. Therefore these performers seem to have been empowered to think that when they come into the interpretive acting area they can do it like they do commercials. So they try, and the end result is shallow and obvious. Or sometimes outright embarrassing.

The trick here, I think, is for the actor to understand what he or she is doing and not confuse the type of work required for one media with the other. I mean there is a difference between playing a character in a play by Eugene O'Neill and doing a thirty-second commercial. You simply don't approach one with the same intensity that you approach the other. That's just common sense. A thirty-second commercial makes certain demands, and as an actor you meet those demands. An O'Neill play requires something completely different.

I personally will do frivolous shit, bad shit, and so forth, commercial shit to make a living, as long as it doesn't impinge on my value system or my moralities as a human being. But that's not what we're talking about. We're talking about what has to remain primary for an artist, the serious intention to illuminate human experience. And that again is what true acting is all about.

But to answer your question, the serious actor approaches these short-term media jobs the same way he or she approaches a job on the stage. With discipline, craft, skill, and an intention to perform in the required situation with all the energy and spontaneity one can muster. That's what being a professional is all about.

FINAL WORDS

Can you sum up for me the gist of our conversations on what it means to be a black actor today?

The one thing a great actor needs is the arrogance to think that what she or he is portraying and the lives they are creating for the stage (or screen) is, if anything, equal to that of anybody else in the world. And the great black actor can only exist with an attitude that the world and consciousness and culture that we come out of is absolutely worthy of being represented up there on the lighted stage. And if anything, we might even have cause to be super-arrogant about it sometimes, because I tend to think we have access to something that's perhaps richer than most other people. Now, I know that that is not strictly true, but I will justify it by saying that because we come from a culture of painful experiences, it tends to equip us with knowing what being human is all about. Consequently, exploring that experience as an artist gives us an endless amount of material from which to grasp some truth concerning the human species that can be investigated intellectually as well as emotionally and then powerfully revealed on stage.

In theatre, as in life, talents are not equal. All of us are not equally talented at everything. Some people have great talents in one area and are absolute idiots or left-footed about other things. Like me when it comes to mechanical appliances or what have you. In those areas I'm not only left-footed but left-handed as well. But in terms of creative talent regarding theatre, I'm on solid ground and would match myself as equal—and sometimes superior—to most people practicing in this area.

So not everyone shares the same degree of talent. But what amount of talent one has can be taken to the maximum in the theatre. And that's what someone wanting to be an actor should strive for. Because as I have always said, I would rather work with somebody who extends their five-minute talent to the limit than deal with someone of greater talent who is marking time or wasting their great potential through laziness, lack of ambition or discipline.

I believe that as actors we must embrace the criterion of "serious intent" as a motivating factor in justifying our participation as performers. We must be convinced of the serious intent of the endeavor. The play, the project, or what have you. A conviction of serious intent justifies our submitting ourselves to the unfettered demands of physical and emotional involvement in the part. Our responsibility then as actors is to use ourselves fully for the illumination of the sum of human behavior. And if we do it honestly, we have to understand that there is nowhere to hide. We are standing there exposed and naked. And this is as it should be. I think great acting takes great courage. And the first step toward that is great commitment.

We talked about acting schools before. Let me say here that the starting point in any training program is that you need a consciously laid out step-by-step process that will ultimately provide you with the tools to do the job. And good acting training at its best will provide you with the ways and means (tools) that will allow you to have a conscious approach to finding the natural ingredients that go into creatively interpreting a character for public presentation and scrutiny.

Acting, at its highest level, is not a skill or a craft that one can do to the ultimate extent unless it's something you absolutely need to do. Something that you need for self-expression in some way that is going to allow you to put in the effort to do it well. And to also be able to stay with it in the face of all the negative frustrations that you might have to face in just trying to be meaningfully employed in your chosen profession. Especially when you're black and have to deal with discouragement coming from so many areas of the society. You can't allow this to stop you. But resisting or trying to be immune from it takes a lot of power and will. And that's why I say it must be something you really need to do.

FINAL WORDS

So here you have it. Some ruminations, remembrances, observations, and determinations about embracing the acting profession and what it means to be a black or African American actor in these times. These are of course not dogmas or rules, but rather meditations and conclusions drawn from a life of working in the theatre in various capacities. They are written down here to provide the aspiring black performer (actor variety) with some guidelines and, yes, advice as to what this profession is all about. And how he or she as an African American person can fit into this spectrum called the American theatre with a full and confident appreciation of our culture, heritage, and strengths.

FINDING THE PLAYS
REFERRED TO IN THE TEXT

The complete scripts of

Ceremonies in Dark Old Men, by Lonne Elder III

A Soldier's Play, by Charles Fuller

The River Niger, by Joseph Walker

The Offering, by Gus Edwards

are in the anthology *Classic Plays from the Negro Ensemble Company,* edited by Paul Carter Harrison and Gus Edwards (1995, University of Pittsburgh Press).

Day of Absence, by Douglas Turner Ward, has been published in tandem with *Happy Ending* (1998, Dramatists Play Service).

Lifetimes on the Streets is part of *Monologues on Black Life,* by Gus Edwards (1997, Heinemann).

The Brownsville Raid, by Charles Fuller, and *Louie and Ophelia,* by Gus Edwards, are not yet published.

MAINSTAGE PLAYS PRODUCED BY THE NEC
UNDER THE ARTISTIC DIRECTION OF
DOUGLAS TURNER WARD

1967–1968
Song of the Lusitanian Bogey, by Peter Weiss
Summer of the Seventeenth Doll, by Raw Lawler
Kongi's Harvest, by Wole Soyinka
Daddy's Goodness, by Richard Wright

1968–1969
God Is a (Guess What?), by Ray Mciver
Ceremonies in Dark Old Men, by Lonne Elder III
Three One-Acts
    String, by Alice Childress
    Contribution, by Ted Shine
    Malcochon, by Derek Walcott
Man Better Man, by Errol Hill

1969–1970
The Harangues, by Joseph A. Walker
Brotherhood, by Douglas Turner Ward
Day of Absence, by Douglas Turner Ward
Akokowe, coordinated by Afolabi Ajayi

1970–1971

Ododo, by Joseph A. Walker

Two One-Acts

    Perry's Mission, by Clarence Young III

    Rosalie Pritchett, by Carlton and Barbara Molette

The Dream on Monkey Mountain, by Derek Walcott

Ride a Black Horse, by John Scott

1971–1972

The Sty of the Blind Pig, by Phillip Hayes Dean

A Ballet Behind the Bridge, by Lennox Brown

Fredrick Douglass . . . Through His Own Words, by Arthur Burghardt

1972–1973

The River Niger, by Joseph A. Walker

1973–1974

The Great Macdaddy, by Paul Carter Harrison

In the Deepest Part of Sleep, by Charles Fuller

1974–1975

The First Breeze of Summer, by Leslie Lee

Waiting for Mungo, by Silas Jones

1975–1976

Eden, by Steve Carter

Livin' Fat, by Judi Ann Mason

1976–1977

The Brownsville Raid, by Charles Fuller

The Great Macdaddy, by Paul Carter Harrison

The Square Root of Soul, by Adolph Caesar

1977–1978

The Offering, by Gus Edwards

Black Body Blues, by Gus Edwards

Twilight Dinner, by Lennox Brown

1978–1979

Nevis Mountain Dew, by Steve Carter

The Daughters of the Mock, by Judi Ann Mason

Everyman/Imprisonment of Obatala (Plays from Africa), by Obotunde Ijimere

A Season to Unravel, by Alexis Deveaux

Old Phantoms, by Gus Edwards

1979–1980

The Michigan, by Dan Owens

Home, by Samm-Art Williams

Lagrima Del Diablo, by Dan Owens

Two One-Acts

    Companions of the Fire, by Ali Wadud

    Big City Blues, by Roy Kuljian

1980–1981

The Sixteenth Round, by Samm-Art Williams

Zooman and the Sign, by Charles Fuller

Weep Not for Me, by Gus Edwards

1981–1982

A Soldier's Play, by Charles Fuller

Colored People's Time (C.P.T.), by Leslie Lee

Abercrombie Apocalypse, by Paul Carter Harrison

1982–1983

Sons and Fathers of Sons, by Ray Arahna

About Heaven and Earth

Three One-Acts

  The Redeemer, by Douglas Turner Ward

  Tigus, by Ali Wadud

  Night Line, by Julie Jensen

Manhattan Made Me, by Gus Edwards

The Isle Is Full of Noise, by Derek Walcott

1983–1984

Puppet Play, by Pearl Cleage

American Dreams, by Velina Houston

Colored People's Time (C.P.T.), by Leslie Lee

1984–1985

District Line, by Joseph L. Walker

Henrietta, by Karen Jones-Meadows

Two Can Play, by Trevor Rhone

Ceremonies in Dark Old Men,
by Lonne Elder III (Classic Series Revival)

1985–1986

Eyes of the American, by Samm-Art Williams

House of Shadows, by Steve Carter

Jonah and the Dog, by Judi Ann Mason

Louie and Ophelia, by Gus Edwards

1986–1987

The War Party, by Leslie Lee

1987–1988

Anchorman, by Paul Carter Harrison

Like Them That Dream, by Edgar White

From the Mississippi Delta, by Dr. Endesha Ids Mae Holland

West Memphis Mojo, Martin Jones

1988–1989

We (four-play cycle), by Charles Fuller
(Reconstruction History Play Series), first two plays

    Prince

    Sally

1989–1990

We (four-play cycle), by Charles Fuller
(Reconstruction History Play Series), final two plays

    Jonquil

    Burners Frolic

Lifetimes on the Streets, by Gus Edwards

1991–1992
The Tommy Parker All-Colored Minstrel Show, by Carlyle Brown

1993
Last Night at Ace's High, by Kenneth Hoke Witherspoon

DOUGLAS TURNER WARD
A CHRONOLOGY

1930   Born on May 5, in Burnside, Louisiana, to Roosevelt and Dorothy (Short) Ward, named Roosevelt Ward, Jr.

1946   Attends Wilberforce University for one year.

1947   Transfers to University of Michigan. Major: Journalism. Plays football as a halfback. After a serious knee injury, he focuses on his interest in politics and theatre.

1948   Moves to NYC. Meets Lorraine Hansberry and Lonne Elder, III. Joins the Progressive Party and becomes a left-wing political activist.

1949   Writes *Star of Liberty*, a short play about the rebellious slave Nat Turner. The play is performed before a political rally of 5,000 people.

        Is arrested and returned to New Orleans where he is imprisoned for three months for draft evasion. His case is appealed.

1951   Lives in New Orleans for two years while the case is pending.

        Writes his first full-length play, *The Trial of Willie McGee*, during this time.

1953   The Supreme Court overturns the draft evasion
        conviction. Moves back to New York.

        Attends Paul Mann's acting workshop and writes for
        the *Daily Worker*, a left-wing political journal.

        At the Hotel Theresa, in Harlem, along with
        Lorraine Hansberry and Lonne Elder III, reads his
        play *The Trial of Willie McGee*.

        Joins the Harlem Writers Workshop.

1958   Gets his first professional acting job, in Eugene
        O'Neill's *The Iceman Cometh*, at the Circle-in-the-
        Square.

        Changes his name to Douglas Turner Ward for acting
        purposes.

1959   Performs a small role in Lorraine Hansberry's *A
        Raisin in the Sun* on Broadway and understudies
        Sidney Poitier as Walter Lee Younger. Meets Robert
        Hooks during the run of the show.

1960   Assumes the lead (Walter Lee Younger) in the
        extended national tour of *A Raisin in the Sun*.

1961   Returns to New York to play Archibald Wellington
        in Jean Genet's *The Blacks*, at St. Mark's Playhouse.

1962   Appears in Thornton Wilder's *Pullman Car
        Hiawatha*.

1963   Appears on Broadway with Kirk Douglas in *One
        Flew Over the Cuckoo's Nest*.

1964   Appears off-Broadway in *The Blood Knot*.

1965   Appears in *Coriolanus,* in Central Park.

His short plays *Happy Ending* and *Day of Absence* open at the St. Mark's Playhouse, produced by Robert Hooks, and win the Vernon Rice Drama Desk Award.

Marries Diana Powell.

1966   Wins two Obie (off-Broadway) awards, one for writing and one for acting, for *Happy Ending* and *Day of Absence.*

Writes an article for the *New York Times* entitled "American Theatre: For Whites Only" (8/14). Because of this article, the Ford Foundation invites Doug Ward, Robert Hooks, and Gerald Krone to submit a proposal for funding to establish a repertory company and training program for black theatre artists.

1967   The Ford Foundation gives Ward, Hooks, and Krone $434,000. The Negro Ensemble Company (NEC) is incorporated, with Robert Hooks as executive director, Gerard Krone as administrative director, and Ward as artistic director.

The company opens its first show, *Song of the Lusitanian Bogey,* by Peter Weiss, to much controversy and acclaim.

A son, Douglas Powell Ward, is born to Diana and Douglas Turner Ward.

1968   Directs his first show, *Daddy Goodness,* by Richard Wright.

Ward and the NEC are publicly accused by the black press of not producing one play by a black American playwright in its first season. Also for using the word *Negro* in its name rather than *black.*

1969   Plays the leading role in Lonne Elder III's *Ceremonies in Dark Old Men* and wins the Drama Desk Award for his performance.

The NEC receives a Tony Award for Special Achievement.

The company is forced to drop its training program due to a shortage of grant monies. Later that year, a benefit at the Winter Garden Theatre saves the NEC from financial collapse.

Robert Hooks leaves the company to pursue other career goals.

1970   *Ceremonies in Dark Old Men* is broadcast in prime time on ABC.

A daughter, Elizabeth Powell Ward, is born to Ward and his wife.

The NEC and Ward are criticized in black periodicals for being located in Greenwich Village instead of Harlem and for retaining a white administrator, Gerry Krone.

1973   Directs and acts in *The River Niger,* by Joseph Walker. This is the first NEC production to move to Broadway.

Receives a Tony Award nomination for best supporting actor but refuses the nomination because his role was not a supporting part—it was the lead.

The play receives a Tony for best play.

1975   *The First Breeze of Summer,* acted in and directed by Ward, moves to Broadway. It receives a best play Tony nomination.

Receives the National Theatre Conference Person-of-the-Year Award.

1977   Is installed in the Louisiana Performing Arts Hall of Fame.

1979   Receives an honorary doctor of fine arts degree from the City College of New York.

Financial setbacks force the NEC to drastically cut back on its staff and its production schedule.

1980   Receives the Ebony Magazine Black American Achievement Award for Accomplishment in Fine Arts.

Directs Samm-Art Williams' play *Home*. The play moves to Broadway and receives two Tony nominations.

The NEC moves from the St. Mark's Theatre, in Greenwich Village, to Theatre Four, on West 54th Street in midtown Manhattan.

1981   Receives the Dr. Martin Luther King Jr. Humanitarian Award for Outstanding Contributions to the Progress of Human Rights.

1982   Directs *A Soldier's Play*, written by Charles Fuller. Fuller receives the Pulitzer Prize for Drama.

Gerald Krone leaves the NEC to work in TV news.

1983   Douglas Turner Ward and Diana Powell Ward divorce.

1984   The NEC gets $100,000 from Citibank but is still facing serious financial troubles.

1987   NEC celebrates its 20th anniversary while facing a major financial shortfall. Ward calls for public support. Some of its announced productions have to be canceled.

Announces his resignation as NEC artistic director, and the title is retired. Leon Denmark is named managing producer.

Is invited by the *New York Times* to write a follow-up article to his "American Theatre: For Whites Only" (8-14-67). When the article, "Counterpoint: A Twenty-Year View of Black Theatre," is submitted, the *Times* refuses to print it. The article is ultimately published in *Black Masks* magazine.

PBS's American Masters series airs a documentary called *The Negro Ensemble Company*, narrated by Ossie Davis.

1990   The NEC announces that it will produce Charles Fuller's ambitious four-play cycle *We*, but financial conditions make this a difficult task.

1991   Receives an honorary doctorate from Columbia College, in Chicago.

Announces in the *New York Times* that the NEC will have to shut down if unable to raise $250,000.

1993   Ward and the NEC are cheered and honored at the National Black Theatre Festival in Winston-Salem, NC, as an "indispensable cultural and national resource."

1996   Is inducted into the Broadway Theatre Hall of Fame on January 22.

Douglas Turner Ward today is semiretired. According to his mood (or interest of the moment), he sometimes conducts acting workshops or gives individual instruction, acts on stage or TV, and occasionally directs. He has received numerous awards for his writing, acting, directing, and contributions to African American and American theatre. Among them are:

Edwin Booth Award (1985)

American Theatre Wing Award (1986)

The NAACP Lifetime Achievement Award (1986)

Honorary Doctorate: Columbia College (1991)

Black Theatre Festival Legacy Award (1991)

Broadway Hall of Fame (1996)

Throughout the African American theatrical community he is affectionately called the godfather of black theatre.

Doug T. Ward as Waters in Charles Fuller's Pulitzer Prize–winning *A Soldier's Play*. Ward did not originate this role but wound up playing it many times. (1984)

I think great acting takes great courage. And the first step toward that is great commitment.

The repertory of black or African American Theatre literature is full of great and interesting characters. Characters that challenge and extend the black actor if he or she puts their mind to it, and makes an honest effort at creating something that is culturally honest.

Gus Edwards and Douglas T. Ward collaborating for the first time in 1977 on Edwards' play *The Offering*. The actors pictured behind are, from left, Kathy Knowles, Charles Weldon, and Olivia Williams.

The great black actor can only exist with an attitude that the world and consciousness and culture that we come out of is absolutely worthy of being represented up there on the lighted stage.

What I'm saying in some ways is acting is a very humane profession.

The black audience is my favorite because they are so responsive, overt, and explicit in their response, they can help you shape your craft.

Douglas Turner Ward and Roxie Roker in Joe Walker's *The River Niger,* the NEC's biggest commercial success.

ABOUT GUS EDWARDS

Gus Edwards is from St. Thomas, Virgin Islands, in the Caribbean. He came to the United States and New York City, where he studied acting (mostly with William Hickey, at the H.B. Studios) and then filmmaking, at the New York Institute of Photography. In 1977 he had his first full-length play, *The Offering*, produced by the Negro Ensemble Company (NEC). Between 1977 and 1993 he had nine plays presented there, making him and Charles Fuller that company's most produced playwrights.

In 1985 he cowrote the television adaptation of James Baldwin's novel *Go Tell It on the Mountain* and in 1988 coauthored the narration for the PBS American Masters documentary *The Negro Ensemble Company*. His plays include:

The Offering (1977)

Black Body Blues (1978)

Old Phantoms (1979)

Weep Not for Me (1981)

Manhattan Made Me (1983)

Moody's Mood Café (1989)

Lifetimes on the Streets (1990)

Restaurant People (1990)

Louie and Ophelia (1991)

Tropicana (1992)

Frederick Douglass (1992)

Testimony (1993)

Confessional (1994)

Dear Martin, Dear Coretta (1995)

Slices (one-acts) (1996)

Black Lives (1996)

Drought Country (1997)

Night Cries (1998)

Black Woman's Blues (1999)

Voices in the Wind (2001)

A Fool Such as I (2002)

Caribbean Babylon (2002)

Snapshots & Duets (2003)

As a playwright, director, and educator, Mr. Edwards has taught at North Carolina School of the Arts, Lehman College (Bronx, NY), Iona College (NY), and Bloomfield College (NJ). Currently he is a tenured professor in the theatre department at Arizona State University, where he teaches film studies and directs a multiethnic theatre program.

He has served on many literary advisory boards and committees, including the Theatre Communications Group, Creative Arts Program Services (NYC), the Artists Foundation (Boston), Hartford Arts Council (CT), New York State Council of the Arts, Arizona Commission of the Arts, Nebraska Arts Council, and the National Endowment for the Arts. He has also served as an Obie (Off-Broadway) Awards judge. He has received playwriting grants from the Rockefeller Foundation, the Drama League, the Arizona Commission of the Arts, and the National Endowment for the Arts.

His published works include *The Offering* and *Old Phantoms* (Dramatists Play Service), *Monologues on Black Life* (Heinemann), *Classic Plays from the Negro Ensemble Company* (coeditor, Pittsburgh University Press), and *More Monologues on Black Life* (Heinemann). His short plays have been published in the anthologies *Lucky 13* (University of Nevada Press), *Center Stage* (University of Illinois Press), and *Best American Short Plays 1996–97* (Applause Books).

His most recent publications include *50 African American Audition Monologues* (Heinemann, 2002) and *Black Theatre: Ritual Performance in the African Diaspora* (coeditor and contributor, Temple University Press, 2002).